GOSPEL

OF THE

SKULL

CRUSHER

THE GLORIOUSLY GOOD NEWS
OF GOD'S PLAN TO FIX EVERYTHING

GOSPEL

OF THE

SKULL

CRUSHER

JOEL RICHARDSON

WINEPRESS
MEDIA

Published by Winepress Media
Book designed by Mark Karis

ISBN: 978-1-949729-25-2

Printed in the United States of America

To Sarah, Kaylee, Ellie, Levi, and Ruby—
my greatest joy in this life.

So you will always know what makes my heart burn
more than anything else.

May you always cling to the hope of His appearing,
and never stop longing for the day when every tear
will be wiped away, and Jesus makes all things new.

CONTENTS

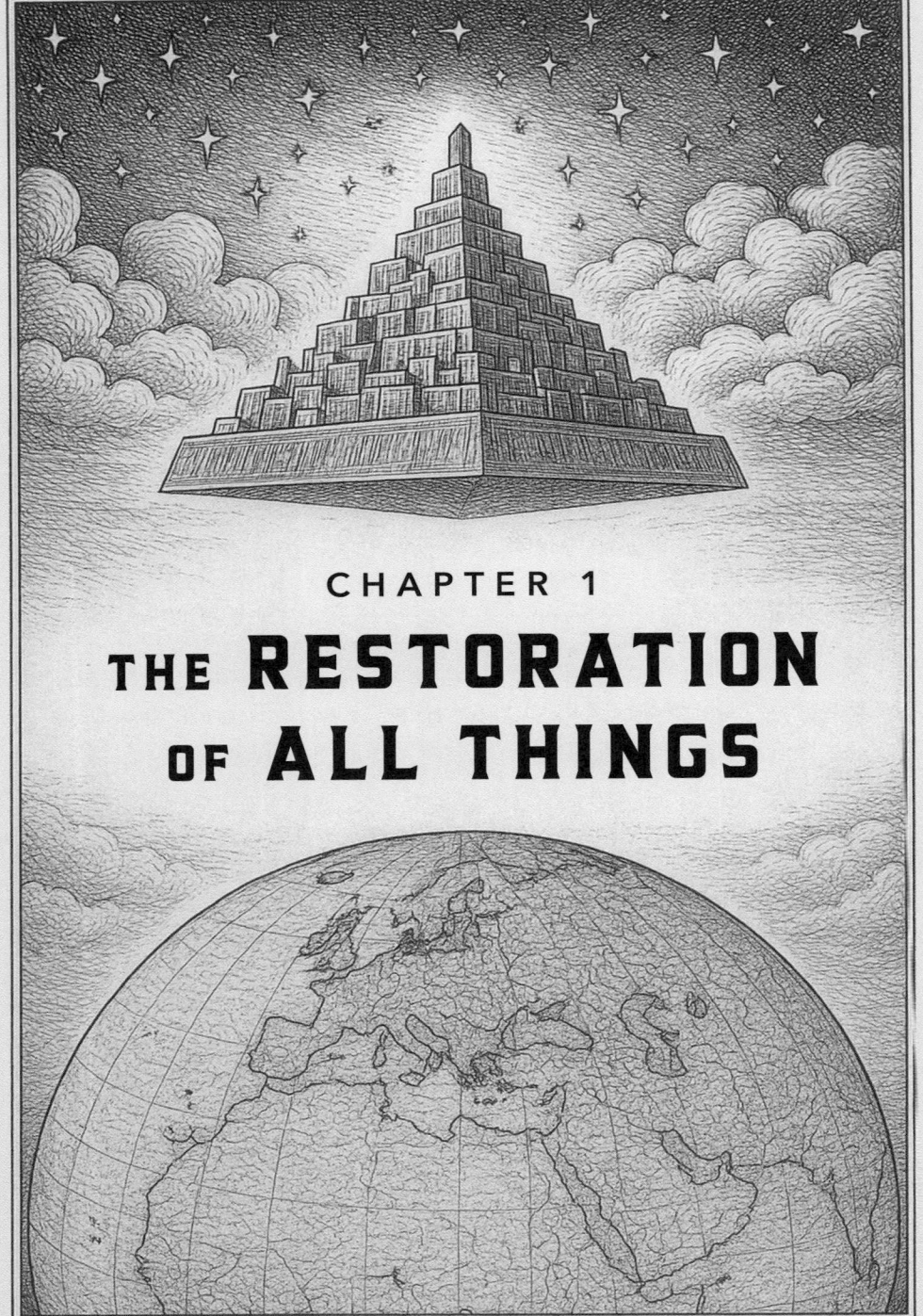

CHAPTER 1

THE **RESTORATION** of **ALL THINGS**

"BEHOLD, I AM MAKING ALL THINGS NEW" (Rev 21:5). In one of the concluding passages of the Bible, while sitting on His throne in heaven, the Lord God Almighty makes this most beautiful declaration. What exactly does God mean when He says He's going to make everything "new"? From Genesis to Revelation, the Bible declares the best news imaginable: the day is coming when God will purify the entire universe from all evil and restore it to its pristine and perfect state, as it was in the beginning. Imagine the paradise of Eden restored, but even better! Both new and improved, far better than the original. The future, as described by the biblical prophets, looks like a paradise kingdom more glorious than we could ever begin to imagine. The best part? The crowning joy is the reality that at that time, Jesus Himself will be physically present, sitting on His "throne of glory" in Jerusalem, reigning as King over all the earth (Matt 19:28). No doubt, some readers will find these descriptions strange, as they are rarely taught in most churches. However, this is precisely what the Bible teaches. There are numerous phrases and ways in which this time is described throughout the pages of Scripture. Jesus Himself described this glorious age in various ways: "the age to come" (Mark 10:30), "the renewal of all things" (Matt 19:28), "my kingdom" (Luke 22:30), and sometimes simply, "the resurrection" (Matt 22:28). The Apostle Peter described it as "the period of restoration of all things about which God spoke by the mouth of His holy prophets from ancient time" (Acts 3:21). The Apostle Paul took it a step further, stating that "the whole creation groans" for this time (Rom 8:22). I find this concept truly fascinating. What does it mean that creation itself is groaning for its own renewal? The reality is that every man, woman, and child has been created with a deep inward longing for a world that is, quite frankly, much better than this one. Whenever I read about the return of Jesus and the many glories to follow, my heart throbs with a yearning so intense that sometimes it hurts. Have you ever felt such a deep longing? There are times when meditating on these things can overwhelm one with emotion. The reason that it resonates so profoundly with everyone who hears it is because this is what we were all created for!

This current, broken, corrupt, tired, and wicked age is not what we were made for. We were made for a better world, for what the whole Bible refers to as "the age to come."

THE END OF THIS WICKED AGE

As profoundly as this vision of a renewed creation resonates within and excites all of our hearts, *it gets even better*. Not only does the Bible promise the restoration of paradise, but it also promises a world cleansed from all corruption and evil. We all sense it: Something is profoundly wrong with the world. Few need to be convinced. While there is certainly tremendous wonder, beauty, and joy to be experienced here and now, the truth is that nearly everything is broken. From politics to the education system, law enforcement, science, the medical world, and even the Church itself—everything is fundamentally tainted and fractured. Far worse, not only are the systems of this world in shambles, but so are we. Corruption is not merely external; it is within all of us.

The simple act of being born guarantees that we will experience sickness, pain, and eventually death. Worse still, we all wrestle with our sins—more than we'd like to admit. Corruption has infiltrated every pocket of the human experience. All of us have stubbornness, pride, and rebellion in our hearts. As Isaiah the prophet said, "We all went astray like sheep; we all have turned to our own way" (Is 53:6). We're all sinners, living in a very broken world. Walking righteously feels like a constant uphill battle, at times exhausting.

This is precisely why God's plan to heal all of creation, *including us*, is such incredibly good news! We all groan for the renewal of all things. We long for a world and a time when the struggle will finally be over. We ache for those coming incandescent days when righteousness, joy, peace, and justice will triumph both outwardly and inwardly.

Imagine a world without all of the struggles we now face. We long for an end to the cosmic loneliness that haunts humanity, when our Creator Himself will live and dwell amongst us forever. We yearn for a different world, one without sickness, death, infidelity, divorce, anxiety,

IN THE BEGINNING

WALKING IN THE GARDEN IN THE COOL OF THE DAY

depression, addiction, overdoses, or suicide. We groan inwardly for a world without dictators, corrupt politicians, predatory ministers, and wars. The list goes on and on. Yes, the Bible declares that all of these things will soon come to an end!

Thus, the good news is double-sided. On the one hand, the Bible promises the restoration of paradise. On the other hand, it also promises the end of everything that makes this age so thoroughly exhausting. When God says, "Behold, I am making all things new," He means it! While God Almighty expressed the gloriously good news, "Behold, I am making all things new," John the Apostle declared the flip side of the coin, stating: "the darkness is passing away" (1 Jn 2:8).

AN ANCHOR OF HOPE

This message has the power to elevate and strengthen us emotionally, significantly affecting how we live and act. When we embrace and internalize it, we find great encouragement for our spirits. I can personally testify to this truth because I've experienced it time and time again. As the writer of Hebrews said, "This hope we have as an anchor of the soul, a hope both sure and steadfast" (Heb 6:19). When the storms of this life rage, the biblical vision of the coming kingdom becomes our unshakable, immovable foundation.

Meditating on this "kingdom that cannot be shaken" (Hebrews 12:28) doesn't just comfort us—it roots us. It stabilizes us. It empowers us to press on. As Hebrews 6:18 says, it is through this hope that we are "greatly encouraged."

The return of Jesus and His kingdom is also one of the most powerful motivators to personal holiness. As the Apostle John wrote: "When He appears, we will be like Him, because we will see Him just as He is. And everyone who has this hope fixed on Him purifies himself, just as He is pure" (1 John 3:2–3).

Today, too many Christians have their minds trapped in the endless cycles of bad news—the latest tragedy, outrage, or scandal. However, we must learn to lift our eyes and redirect our attention to the good news.

The darkness will not last forever. The dawn is coming.

Among all of the various visions of the future, all of the religious or philosophical narratives that mankind has to offer, nothing is more encouraging to the human heart. It is for this reason and so many others that this story needs to be told. We must be deliberate about regularly encouraging one another with this hope, "all the more as you see the day drawing near" (Heb 10:25).

RECOVERING THE GOOD NEWS

Ask most Christians what "the Gospel" is, and you'll typically hear a message about how to be saved. But rarely do we hear what we are saved unto. When asked what the Gospel is, they will often cite John 3:16 and stop there.

Many tend to believe that the good news is little more than this: become a Christian, and after you die, you escape hell and will go to heaven forever. While the Bible does teach that the souls of the righteous who've died are presently with Jesus, it does not teach that the faithful will become disembodied souls in some spiritual plane, forever. Jesus didn't die merely to save our souls; He came to redeem all things, both in heaven and on the earth (Ephesians 1:10).

Although the return of the King and the establishment of His Kingdom is the primary focus of all expectation, longing, and hope throughout the entire Bible, today, such hope is rarely preached in the churches. The cry of the early Church was powerful and hopeful: "*Maranatha!*" The cry of the early Church was not simply "Hallelujah" (Praise the Lord), but also, "Come Lord Jesus!" The Apostle Peter went so far as to exhort all believers to emphatically, "fix your hope completely on the grace to be brought to you at the revelation of Jesus Christ" (1 Peter 1:13). Why have we strayed from this cry for Jesus's return? How have God's people strayed so far from the simplicity of this cry for the return of Jesus and the glorious kingdom He will establish?

The good news is that the Maranatha cry is returning. At the end of the Book of Revelation, the Apostle John foresaw the last-days Church united in one voice, crying out, "Come!" (Revelation 22:17). Even now, the Church is beginning to reclaim the fullness of the Gospel—and with it, the Maranatha cry that echoes and resounds down through the ages: *Come, Lord Jesus!*

CHAPTER 2
THE HUMILIATED
DUST LICKER

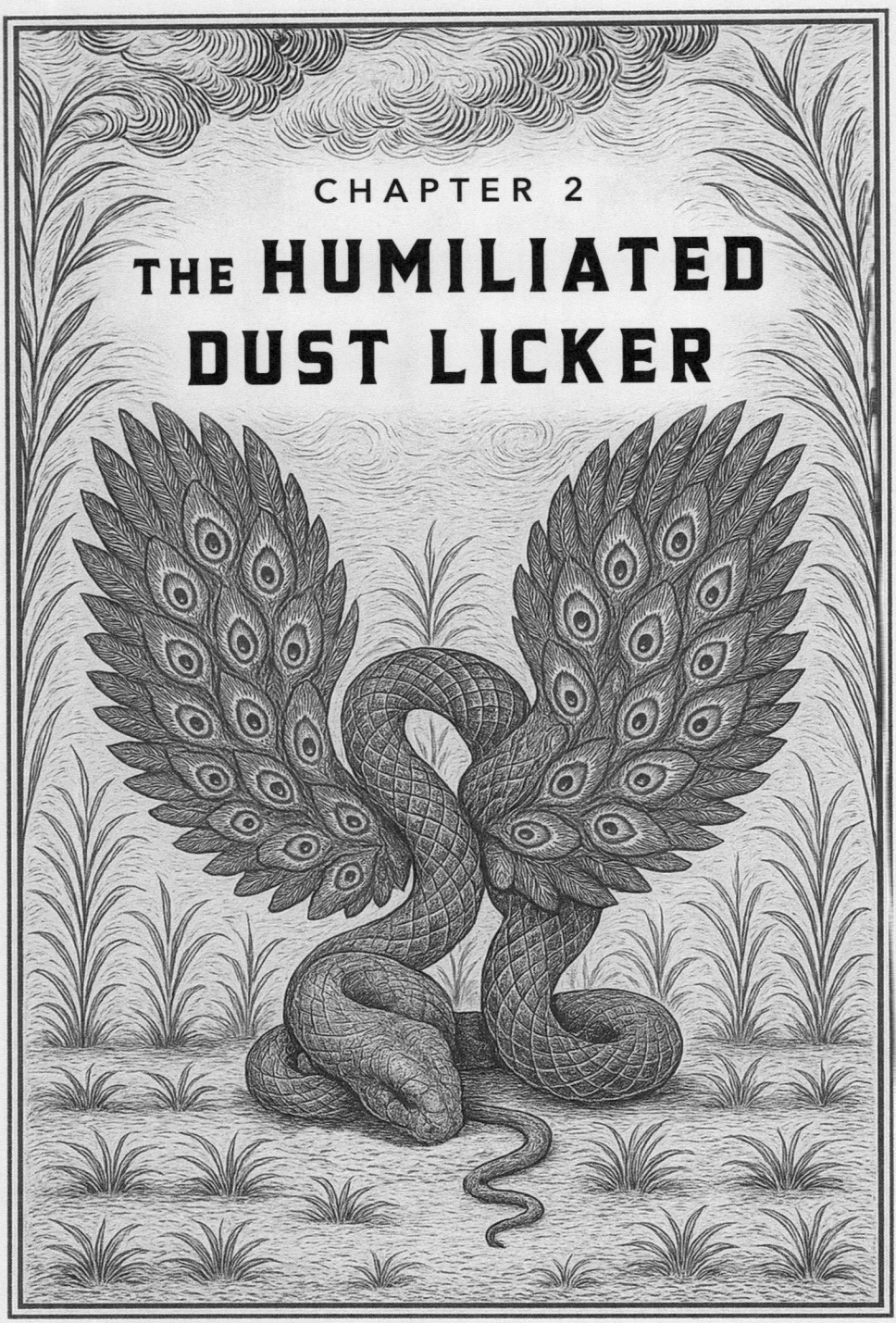

PARADISE RESTORED. This is the glowing hope that the Bible promises. The book you are holding represents a journey. Together, we will trace the golden thread of God's promises as it weaves its way throughout the pages of Scripture. As we will see, from the very first chapters in Genesis to the closing words in Revelation, the glorious news of God's plan to restore paradise is firmly established.

So, if the world was so perfect in the beginning, what happened? How did we get to where we are now? How did everything become so incredibly broken, corrupt, and painful? Most Christians, when asked why the world is so messed up, point to the story of Adam and Eve and their disobedience in the garden—"The Fall," as we call it. While the curses God unleashed in the garden certainly play a significant role in why this world is such an absolute mess, there's much more to the story. The Bible tells of multiple rebellions against God, all of which have led to the shattered condition of the world we now inhabit. What does the Bible say about these ancient rebellions?

THE REBELLION OF SATAN

Long before Adam and Eve ate from the forbidden tree, there was another rebellion—a heavenly one. Behind the serpent's deception in the garden stood a figure far more ancient and cunning: a majestic being sometimes called Lucifer, which means "shining one," "morning star," or "son of the dawn." Satan was not created as the devil we know today. Instead, he began as one of the most exalted heavenly beings in God's court.

Ezekiel describes him this way:

> "You had the seal of perfection, full of wisdom and perfect in beauty... You were the anointed cherub who covers, and I placed you there. You were on the holy mountain of God; You walked in the midst of the stones of fire. You were blameless in your ways from the day you were created until unrighteousness was found in you" (Ezekiel 28:12–15).

SATAN, THE CHERUB

He was adorned with radiant "perfect" beauty and empowered with great authority. He walked among the "stones of fire," indicating his nearness to the very throne of God. But this magnificence was not enough. Pride filled his heart, and rather than worshiping God, he sought to be worshiped as God.

Isaiah captures the arrogant ambition within him that led to his ruin:

> "You said in your heart, 'I will ascend to heaven; I will raise my throne above the stars of God, and I will sit on the mount of assembly ... I will ascend above the heights of the clouds; I will make myself like the Most High. Nevertheless you will be thrust down to Sheol, to the recesses of the pit" (Isaiah 14:13–15).

Pride led to rebellion. From the heights of heaven to the depths of disgrace. Once a guardian of the glory of God, he is now the father of lies (John 8:44), the accuser (Rev 12:10), and the deceiver of nations.

Thus, even before Adam and Eve fell, Satan had already rebelled. As the first of the rebels, the operation in the garden to deceive Adam and Eve was part of Satan's effort to drag the whole world down with him, to pull everyone under his control. Today, Satan has such an influence over the peoples of the earth that Jesus referred to him as "the ruler of this world" (John 12:31) and Paul the Apostle called him, "the god of this age" (2 Co 4:3–4). John the Apostle said, "The whole world lies in the power of the evil one" (1 Jn 5:19).

So, how did Satan manage to acquire so much power over the people of this planet? This brings us to the most tragic story of Adam and Eve and the fall of mankind.

IT WAS VERY GOOD

After God created the heavens and the earth, the plants, and the animals, He made mankind. Then, "God saw all that He had made, and behold, it was very good" (Gen 1:31). It wasn't just good; it was *amazing*. Absolute paradise. Its centerpiece was "the garden toward the east, in

Eden" (Gen 2:8), the home God prepared for Adam and Eve. In stark contrast to the Bible's opening scenes of darkness and chaotic waters, the world was now well-ordered and bursting with exquisite beauty. God caused every tree that was pleasing to the sight and good for food to grow there (Gen 2:9). Chief among them was "the tree of life" (Gen 2:9). There in paradise, Adam and Eve lived without shame, sickness, or death. There was only one command to obey: do not eat from "the tree of the knowledge of good and evil" (Gen 2:17). The consequences were clear: "in the day that you eat from it you will surely die" (Gen 2:17).

THE SERPENT

As the story unfolds, in the midst of this perfection, a serpent appears: "Now the serpent was more crafty than any beast of the field which the Lord God had made. And it said to the woman, 'Indeed, has God said, "You shall not eat from any tree of the garden"?'" (Gen 3:1). Who or what exactly was this serpent?

On one hand, the serpent is grouped alongside other common animals (Gen 2:19; 3:1,14). On the other hand, this entity possessed intelligence greater than man's and could speak. This was no ordinary reptile. The Hebrew word translated as "serpent" is *nachash*. While often used for snakes, it also appears in Job and Isaiah to describe the great sea creature, Leviathan—"the fleeing serpent" (Job 26:13), and "the twisted serpent" (Isa 27:1).

In the final book of the Bible, Revelation identifies the serpent as Satan: "the great dragon... the serpent of old who is called the devil and Satan, who deceives the whole world" (Rev 12:9; 20:2). Paul the Apostle agrees. In 2 Corinthians 11, he warns, "As the serpent deceived Eve by his craftiness, your minds will be led astray from the simplicity and purity of devotion to Christ" (2 Cor 11:3), and adds, "For even Satan disguises himself as an angel of light" (2 Cor 11:14). Paul's point is clear: the serpent in the garden was Satan—a rebellious divine being who had disguised himself by taking on the appearance of a serpent.

THE DECEPTION OF ADAM AND EVE

THE REBELLION AND FALL OF MAN

Most of us know the story. Satan's scheme succeeded. After being manipulated by the deceiver, Adam and Eve disobeyed:

> "When the woman saw that the tree was good for food, and that it was a delight to the eyes, and that the tree was desirable to make one wise, she took from its fruit and ate; and she gave also to her husband with her, and he ate" (Genesis 3:6).

With that act, chaos returned. It was the greatest catastrophe in human history.

Mankind, created in God's image to rule the world, had fallen. Every human from that day forward would be born into a life saturated with pain and death. Rather than walking in perfect communion with their creator, now Adam and Eve felt something very new: shame. The unbroken communion they'd previously enjoyed with their Creator was now fundamentally fractured, and they knew it. When the Lord next returned to see them, they hid. Mankind plunged headlong into the current corrupt state that we now find ourselves in. We all live far from paradise, far from unbroken fellowship with God, every one of us slouching toward the grave.

THE CURSE OF ADAM: MANKIND'S NEW PAINFUL REALITY

Adam and Eve's sin affected everything. Not only was their relationship with God fractured, but they also lost access to paradise. God expelled them from the Garden and from the Tree of Life (Gen 3:23). To guard the way back, He stationed cherubim and a flaming sword (Gen 3:24). Beyond losing eternal life, the new human reality included suffering. To Eve, God said childbirth would now come through great pain (Gen 3:16). To Adam, He said:

> "Cursed is the ground because of you; In toil you will eat of it all the days of your life. Both thorns and thistles it shall grow for you;

ADAM AND EVE EXPELLED FROM PARADISE

THE NEPHILIM

And you will eat the plants of the field. By the sweat of your face You will eat bread, Till you return to the ground, Because from it you were taken; For you are dust, And to dust you shall return" (Genesis 3:17–19).

Now, even obtaining food would require painful labor. The very earth was cursed. Life became a ceaseless grind until death returned humanity to the dust. From that point forward, every man or woman who has ever been born would end their journey with death.

THE REBELLION OF THE SONS OF GOD AND THE NEPHILIM

As if all of this were not bad enough, the tragedy deepens. Beyond the rebellion of the devil and the fall of all mankind, the Bible also tells of another profound ancient spiritual rebellion when many powerful heavenly beings—"sons of God"—agreed to "abandon their proper abode" and have children with "the daughters of men" (cf., Jd 6, Gen 6:2; 1 En 6-7). This resulted in a hybrid race of particularly wicked and extraordinarily large beings. A mixed race of giants now shared this planet with humankind. The Bible calls them "the Nephilim." These giants are described as "the mighty men who were of old, men of renown." (Gen 6:4). While most are familiar with the story of Goliath the giant who David killed, few are aware that much of the Old Testament story of Israel conquering the promised land revolves around their many battles against these giant clans who were living in the land of Canaan.

THE DUST LICKER: SATAN'S HUMILIATION FORETOLD

With the horror of humanity's new cursed reality still fresh, God reinserted Himself into the story, unveiling His plan to fix what had been broken. First, He cursed Satan, the ringleader of the rebellion. The Hebrew text is rich with poetic irony. The serpent, initially described as "crafty" (*arum*), becomes "cursed" (*arur*) above all animals (Gen 3:14). He would crawl on his belly and eat dust—an image of total defeat.

Micah echoes this language:

"They will lick the dust like a serpent, Like reptiles of the earth. They will come trembling out of their fortresses; To the Lord our God they will come in dread And they will be afraid before You" (Micah 7:17).

Even during the future millennial reign of Jesus, we read, "The wolf and the lamb will graze together... but dust will be the serpent's food" (Isa 65:25). From the very beginning, God foretold Satan's humiliation. Once the anointed cherub, he is now the humiliated dust-licker. God declared the end from the beginning.

PARADISE FALLEN. PARADISE RESTORED.

So begins the story. First, a glimpse of the world as it once was—a sublime garden paradise. Then we watch in horror as that perfection was corrupted, defiled, and shattered. Instead of Eden, humanity's experience is now marked by unavoidable painful childbirth, difficult labor, hard ground, thorns and briars—and in the end, death. But we are not left without hope. Next, we will begin to discover the Lord's glorious plans to fix everything. *Renewal, restoration, redemption*—it is to these themes that we now eagerly turn our attention.

CHAPTER 3

THE SKULL CRUSHER

IMMEDIATELY AFTER THE LORD CURSED THE SERPENT, His following statement introduced the absolute best news imaginable. It is the first prophecy in the Bible that predicts the coming of the Messiah, and it serves as the foundation for all subsequent messianic prophecies. Theologians sometimes refer to the Lord's declaration here as "the first Gospel" or "the mother prophecy." In this single verse, we find a prophetic glimpse not only of the coming of the Messiah but also of the cross, the Antichrist, the Lord's victory at the Battle of Armageddon, and the restoration of paradise. While this information is only found in a minimal form here, it is the seed of revelation from which many other foundational truths sprout. It is here that God's plan of redemption is first introduced. The prophetic announcement begins:

> "And I will put enmity Between you and the woman, And between your seed and her seed; He shall bruise you on the head, And you shall bruise him on the heel." (Genesis 3:15)

Throughout the entire Bible, there are few verses in which so much revelation is packed into such a small space. In a single sentence, we have an overview of the entirety of the Lord's plans to redeem creation, to fix everything. Let's pause to consider the primary components of this plan.

ENMITY

When the serpent entered the garden with a premeditated plan to deceive and corrupt mankind, he started a war. With the words "I will put enmity between you and the woman," the Lord made it clear that although Satan started the war, He would finish it. There would be no turning the other cheek, no extension of mercy. Instead, the Lord chose to meet violence with violence, declaring a perpetual war between the righteous and the wicked.

We see this struggle unfold throughout the pages of the Bible; it has played out on the world stage throughout human history, and it continues to rage before us all at this very moment.

Those who follow the ways of Satan have been—and continue to be—at war with God's people and God's plan of redemption. The Lord's means of fighting this war: He will raise up a righteous seed-line from which will come "the seed."

SEED-LINES

The word translated as "seed" is sometimes rendered "descendants" or "offspring." In Hebrew, the word is *zera*. The same word is used for both the singular and plural. In this prophecy, it is both. From Eve and the serpent would come two distinct seed-lines. They are not literal but metaphorical. Satan has never literally fathered physical children, and the prophecy does not speak of a clash between two ethnic groups or genetic lines.

This point must be emphasized because some have wrongly interpreted this passage, leading to some truly racist doctrines that frame particular ethnic groups as the literal children of the Devil. No humans are roaming the earth literally carrying Satan's DNA. There are, however, a multitude who imitate him and follow his ways. The intention of this passage is to speak of the metaphorical or spiritual children of the evil one. The Bible understands those who follow the ways of Satan to be his "children." Jesus Himself expressed this when He rebuked some religious leaders, saying: "You are doing the deeds of your father... You are of your father the devil, and you want to do the desires of your father. He was a murderer from the beginning" (John 8:41, 44).

THE BATTLE BETWEEN THE SEED-LINES

So, the prophecy tells us that two groups are at war—those who follow the ways of the Lord versus those who follow the ways of Satan. This war will reach its climax when an ultimate representative from each line emerges and the two face off in a final battle at the end of this age.

At first, the prophecy doesn't tell us much about this righteous seed. It simply says "he." He is a male individual. Christians look back and understand this to be a prophecy about Jesus the Messiah.

THE WAR BETWEEN TWO SEED LINES

THE HUMILATION OF THE SERPENT

From the wicked seed-line will come an individual known by many titles, the most well-known of which is "the Antichrist." Thus, the long historical battle between God and Satan, between God's children and Satan's children, will be settled when two men—Jesus the Messiah and the Antichrist—face one another in a final decisive clash.

The fight, however, is no equal match—it is a profoundly lopsided battle. Whereas the serpent would merely strike his opponent's foot, the Righteous Seed would stomp the head. Both the heel and head injuries are metaphors. The "bruising of the heel" is a poetic reference to Jesus' suffering on the cross; the "crushing of the head" represents the serpent's ultimate humiliation and defeat. After thousands of years of warfare and deceit, the lowly dust-licker will meet his ignoble end—utterly defeated and eternally damned.

But when? When will Satan suffer this death blow? The Bible tells us that it is unfolding right now. First, it was sealed and guaranteed at the cross. It will be more fully realized at Armageddon when Jesus returns to defeat the Antichrist and his armies. After that, Satan himself will be bound in chains and thrown into the abyss for a thousand years:

> "Then I saw an angel coming down from heaven, holding the key of the abyss and a great chain in his hand. And he laid hold of the dragon, the serpent of old, who is the devil and Satan, and bound him for a thousand years; and he threw him into the abyss, and shut it and sealed it over him, so that he would not deceive the nations any longer, until the thousand years were completed" (Revelation 20:1–3).

Finally, after the thousand years are complete, then "the devil [will be] thrown into the lake of fire and brimstone… [to be] tormented day and night forever and ever" (Revelation 20:10). Paul the apostle describes it this way: "that lawless one… [who] the Lord will slay with the breath of His mouth and bring to an end by the appearance of His coming" (2 Thessalonians 2:8).

So, is it the serpent or the Antichrist who will have their head

THE SKULL CRUSHER

crushed? The answer is both. The Antichrist is essentially Satan's human puppet, the earthly vessel through which he will attempt to carry out his plans on earth. In slaying the Antichrist, Jesus delivers a decisive blow to Satan himself. The final end, as we just read, occurs when Satan is finally cast into the lake of fire.

JESUS, THE DIVINE WARRIOR

The fact that the Bible foresees Jesus as violent is no doubt shocking to some. Many have been raised to view Jesus as a kind of Jewish guru-like figure whose teachings were purely passive and non-violent. But that is not the case. Whereas the Messiah is introduced at the beginning of the Bible as a wounded yet victorious warrior, the Bible concludes by portraying Jesus as a divine warrior who will crush, defeat, and slay his enemies and the enemies of his people. In one of the final chapters of the Bible, after He is described as the One whose words are like a sharp sword, it is said that "in righteousness He judges and wages war" (Revelation 19:11). As we will see, this theme is the most common and consistent way Jesus and His mission are described throughout the Bible. Jesus is the divine warrior—the serpent-slaying skull crusher.

CONCLUSION

In just the third chapter of the Bible, Satan's defeat is declared with certainty. As soon as Adam and Eve sinned, as soon as death entered the world, God introduced His solution, His plan of redemption. To answer the enmity of the Serpent and his children, the Lord would raise up a people, a seed-line from which the ultimate Seed would come. In this prophecy, we glimpse the Messiah's future suffering on the cross, His future triumph over the Antichrist, and His eventual victory over Satan himself. Here in the garden, the seed of messianic hope was planted. It is from this ancient promise that God's redemptive plan will sprout. It is from this kernel that the full gospel proclaimed by Jesus and the apostles finds its origin. Today, this ancient promise remains a beacon of hope for all humanity.

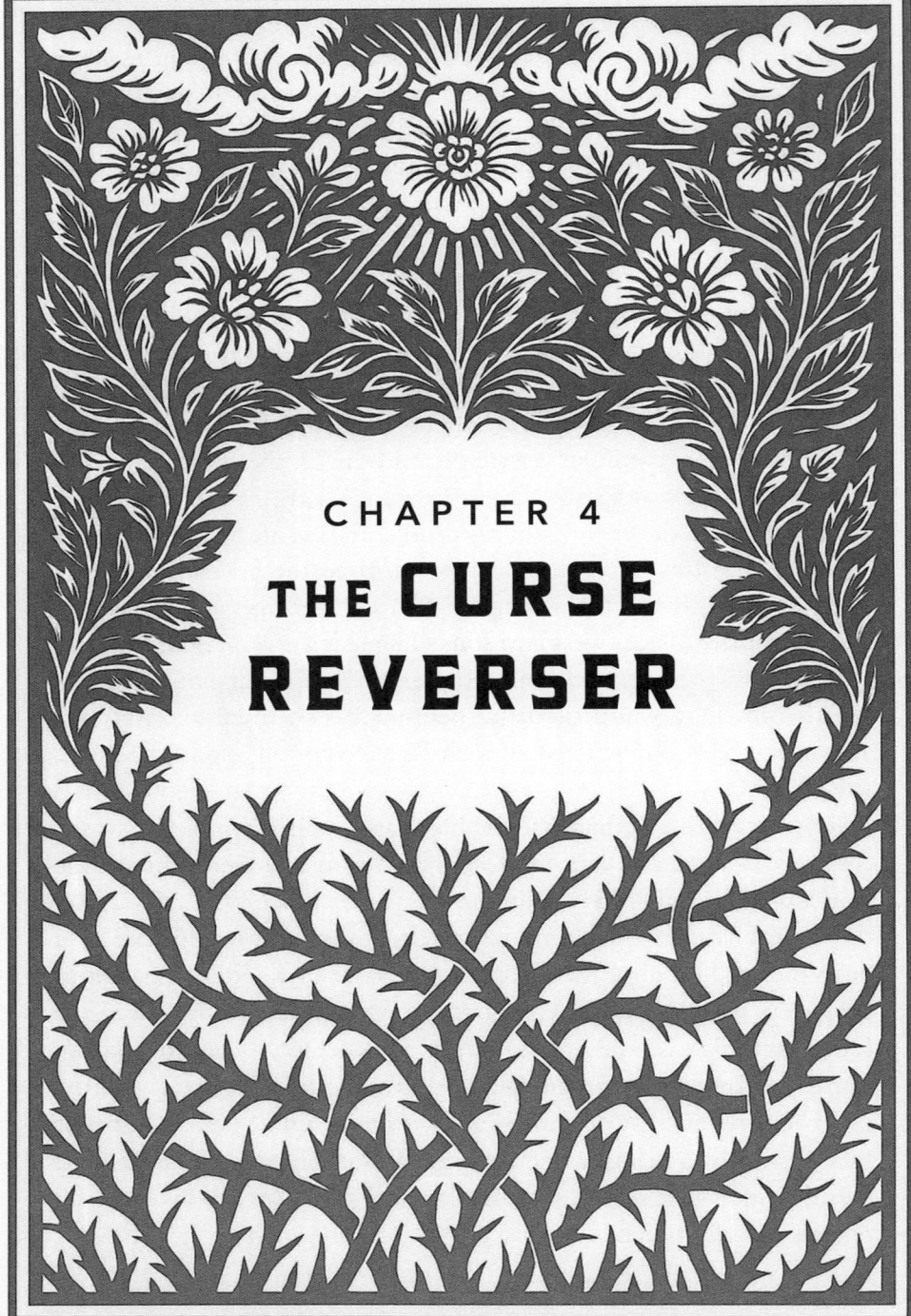

CHAPTER 4

THE CURSE REVERSER

THUS, THE STORY OF ALL STORIES BEGINS. Having lived in unbroken fellowship with their Creator, enjoying paradise, the mother and father of mankind now experienced a completely different life, outside the garden.

I'm sure many reading this can relate to living with regret. Now, imagine how Adam and Eve felt after the fall. Up to that point, they had only known absolute, idyllic perfection. Then, in an instant, they felt the weight of the curse and, no doubt, unfathomable sorrow, perhaps for many long centuries!

So, when the Lord promised that a male child would come—one who would reverse the curse and restore paradise—there can be little doubt that every time a baby boy was born, Adam and Eve, with hearts full of hopeful desperation, asked, "Could this be the One?"

THE RIGHTEOUS AND THE UNRIGHTEOUS SEED-LINES

Almost immediately after the announcement of the two seed-lines and their perpetual enmity, the Bible tells the story of Cain and Abel, Adam and Eve's first two sons. The elder, Eve named Cain. In the biblical world, names were chosen with meaning. The Hebrew verb *qaniti*, from which the name Cain is derived, means "gotten" or "brought forth." Thus, Eve declared, "I have gotten a manchild with the help of the Lord" (Gen. 4:1). This suggests that Eve may have believed, or perhaps hoped, that Cain was the Promised One—the Skull Crusher. Of course, if those were her expectations, she would be quickly and painfully disappointed.

Cain became a gardener, while his younger brother Abel raised animals. Both brought the fruit of their labor to God as an offering. But while Abel's sacrifice was accepted, Cain's was not. According to Jewish tradition, fire from heaven consumed Abel's offering, while Cain's received no such sign. What was the difference?

The Bible says Abel offered "the firstlings of his flock and of their fat portions" (Gen. 4:4). He gave the first and best, acknowledging that everything belonged to God. Furthermore, the New Testament tells us that Abel offered his sacrifice "by faith," whereas Cain did not

(Heb. 11:4, 6). The rest of the story is incredibly dark. Overcome with jealousy and rage, Cain murdered his brother.

Perhaps this is why Jesus would later teach that harboring anger and hatred toward one's brother is equivalent to murder (Matt. 5:21–22). Far from being the Promised One, Cain revealed himself to be the first representative of the unrighteous seed-line—the spiritual children of Satan.

The hostility between Cain and Abel—between the unrighteous and the righteous—is a theme woven throughout Scripture that continues to play out, even today, on the world stage. As noted in the previous chapter, though righteousness and wickedness often manifest within tribal or family lines, at their core, they are always spiritual—matters of the heart. The Bible offers many examples of righteous individuals emerging from wicked backgrounds, and vice versa. Even Cain was given a chance to do what was right:

> "Why are you angry? Why is your face downcast? If you do what is right, will you not be accepted? But if you do not do what is right, sin is crouching at your door; it desires to have you, but you must rule over it." (Genesis 4:6–7)

Cain rejected the Lord's offer of grace, choosing instead to follow his darker inclinations. Abel's blood was spilled, and Cain was "driven… from the presence of the Lord" (Gen. 4:16).

THE LINE OF SETH

Genesis 4 then shifts focus to other children of Adam and Eve who lived righteously and who "by faith… gained approval" from God (Heb. 11:2). The birth of Seth filled the void left by Abel's death. Eve then said, "God has appointed me another offspring in place of Abel, for Cain killed him" (Gen. 4:25). The righteous line would now be reckoned through the line of Seth. It was during the days of Seth's son Enosh that we read: "Then men began to call upon the name of the LORD" (v. 26).

CAIN KILLS ABEL

ENOCH

Genesis 5 follows the male descendants of the righteous line of Seth: from Enosh to Kenan, Mahalalel, Jared, and then Enoch. While earlier generations had begun to call on the name of the Lord, Enoch went further. The Bible says that he actually "walked with God" (vv. 22, 24) and then he just kept on walking. So intimately did he walk with God that the Bible says, "God took him." The Epistle to the Hebrews adds:

> "By faith Enoch was taken up so that he would not see death; and he was not found because God took him up; for he obtained the witness that before his being taken up he was pleasing to God." (Hebrews 11:5)

This is powerful. Though all humanity was sentenced to death through Adam's fall, Enoch somehow found a door of escape through intimate fellowship with God. At the time of his translation into heaven, Adam had already died of old age. Seth, Enosh, Kenan, Mahalalel, Jared, Methuselah, and Lamech were all still alive. It's very possible they witnessed Enoch's departure. Imagine the impression it left on that generation.

Even more significant is what the New Testament says Enoch *prophesied*:

> "Behold, the Lord came with many thousands of His holy ones, to execute judgment upon all, and to convict all the ungodly of all their ungodly deeds which they have done in an ungodly way…" (Jude 14–15)

This is a prophecy about the second coming of the Messiah. Remarkably, even before the flood—just seven generations from Adam—there was already an awareness and understanding that the Promised One would not only be "the seed," born of a woman, but would also come from heaven as God Almighty with myriads of angels to judge the earth.

Here is one of the first and greatest mysteries in the Bible: how can the

ENOCH'S VISION

Promised One be born naturally as a human, yet also come from heaven as God, the Divine Judge? Surely the early righteous believers would have wrestled with this. It is truly astounding to consider that many of those who lived a mere seven generations from Adam had a solid understanding that someday, the Savior would come from heaven with an army of angels to judge the wicked. It is no surprise, then, that the writer of Hebrews referred back and included these earliest believers when he said, "All these died in faith, without receiving the promises, but having seen them and having welcomed them from a distance" (Heb 11:13).

The ancient righteous ones understood a lot more than we often give them credit for.

THE ONE WHO WILL GIVE US REST

Another truly beautiful part of God's prophetic declaration is the theme of paradise restored. The good news of God's promise was not simply that Satan will one day be crushed. Yes, that the enemy of God and humanity will eventually be forever silenced is terrific news, of course. But within the promise to bruise the serpent's head is also the promise to undo all the pain, toil, and suffering that entered the world through the curse. The crushing of the serpent's head entails the reversal of everything that came through his deception. The hope offered in this prophecy is not merely the end of Satan, but the complete reversal of the curse—the restoration of Eden.

The declaration doesn't state this outright, but we do witness its expectation among the righteous who lived before the flood. We see it clearly in the story of Noah's birth.

After Enoch came Methuselah, Lamech, and then Noah. Of Lamech it is written:

> "Lamech lived one hundred and eighty-two years, and became the father of a son. Now he called his name Noah, saying, 'This one will give us rest from our work and from the toil of our hands arising from the ground which the LORD has cursed.'" (Genesis 5:28–29)

The name *Noah* means "rest" or "comfort." Lamech expected that the Promised One would bring rest and relief from the agony of the curse. His direct reference to painful toil and cursed ground makes that expectation clear.

Since Eden, humanity had been condemned to eke out a living by the sweat of their brows. But Lamech foresaw the day when the curse would be reversed. The Coming One wouldn't only crush the serpent—He would also lift the curse, restore creation, and remove death's dominion over the righteous.

The Promised One would be a warrior, yes—but He would be far more. He would be the Redeemer, the Healer, and the Restorer of all things. He would be the Curse-Reverser.

THE SEED-LINE OF SHEM

Genesis 6 recounts another key episode that identifies the next bearer of the promised line. Most know the story of the flood: the earth was filled with violence, and God determined to judge it:

> "Now the earth was corrupt in the sight of God, and the earth was filled with violence … Then God said to Noah, 'The end of all flesh has come before Me… behold, I am about to destroy them with the earth.'" (Genesis 6:11–13)

God commanded Noah to build the ark through which his family and a remnant of creation would be saved. After the flood, Noah and his sons; Shem, Ham, and Japheth exited the ark. Then we read:

> "Then Noah began farming and planted a vineyard. He drank of the wine and became drunk… Ham… saw the nakedness of his father and told his two brothers… But Shem and Japheth took a garment… and covered the nakedness of their father…" (Genesis 9:18–23)

When Noah awoke, he pronounced a prophetic curse, not on Ham, but on Ham's son, Canaan. This poetic curse, or heptastich, has a triadic structure, which repeats the curse three times:

"Cursed be Canaan; A servant of servants He shall be to his brothers."

"Blessed be the LORD, The God of Shem; And let Canaan be his servant."

"May God enlarge Japheth, And let him dwell in the tents of Shem; And let Canaan be his servant." (Genesis 9:25–27)

Most important here is that Shem is singled out. First, the Lord is declared to be *his* God. Then it is said that God Himself will *dwell* in Shem's tents.

Thus, following Seth, Enoch, Noah, and other righteous men, Shem is revealed as the next in the line of promise. Through him the Seed would come—the One who would crush the serpent, reverse the curse, and bring the righteous the rest they've long yearned for.

CHAPTER 5

THE **SEED** OF **ABRAHAM**

AS WE FOLLOW THE GOLDEN THREAD of messianic expectation, it leads us next to the story of Abraham.

Here, the seed of messianic hope planted in the garden vigorously sprouts up through the soil. Because the condemnation of the serpent came from the mouth of God, it is a divinely guaranteed prophecy. In the story of Abraham, God formalizes these promises through a very solemn covenant. The promises God made to Abraham are among the most foundational and essential in the entire Bible. They are also the very hinge upon which much of world history has turned. If we wish to understand the primary spiritual dynamic behind the most significant geopolitical conflict in the world today, what Isaiah calls "the controversy of Zion" (Isaiah 34:8)—the controversy between the State of Israel and practically every other nation—then we must first understand God's covenant with Abraham.

THE ABRAHAMIC COVENANT

It all began when the Lord spoke to Abram (whose name would later be changed to Abraham), calling him to leave his homeland:

> "Now the Lord said to Abram, 'Go forth from your country, and from your relatives and from your father's house, to the land which I will show you'" (Genesis 12:1).

So Abraham left Ur of the Chaldeans (Gen 11:31; 15:7), a city located in what is now southeastern Turkey. As the Lord looked down upon a world filled with rebellion and violence, His plan to redeem it all began through the simple act of calling one man to leave behind his family, his home, and everything familiar.

For anyone who has left family or homeland in obedience to the Lord's calling, this story resonates deeply, especially those called to serve Him in foreign lands. As the book of Hebrews says:

> "By faith Abraham, when he was called, obeyed by going out to a place which he was to receive for an inheritance; and he went out, not knowing where he was going" (Hebrews 11:8).

A GREAT BLESSING TO ALL NATIONS

With the call to leave came a profound promise: the Lord would multiply Abraham's descendants so that they would become a great people. Through them, He would bring blessings to the entire world:

> "And I will make you a great nation, And I will bless you, And make your name great; And so you shall be a blessing; And I will bless those who bless you, And the one who curses you I will curse. And in you all the families of the earth will be blessed" (Genesis 12:2–3).

THE PROMISED LAND

After Abraham entered the land of Canaan (modern-day Israel), the Lord promised to give that very land to his descendants:

> "The Lord appeared to Abram and said, 'To your descendants I will give this land'" (Genesis 12:7).

Many who love Israel often quote the first part of the promise—"I will bless those who bless you, and the one who curses you I will curse"—but they frequently leave out the rest: "And in you all the families of the earth will be blessed." Both aspects of the promise are crucial. Yes, the Lord chose Abraham's descendants and promised them the land, but His ultimate purpose was to bring blessing to every nation on earth.

It may sound paradoxical: that God, in loving every nation, chose to single out one nation and one land. But Israel's unique role is not about favoritism. Instead, Israel was chosen as the vessel through which God would bring redemption to the world. Think of Israel as God's launching pad—His strategic base of operations—from which He would bless every tribe, tongue, and nation. The Lord chose the Promised Land as His base, His beachhead, for the redemption of the world.

This is why so many of today's geopolitical conflicts revolve around Israel. They are the visible outworking of a deeper, spiritual conflict

SO SHALL YOUR DESCENDANTS BE

being waged over this land and these people (Eph 6:12). If God is finished with Israel, then it is clear that Satan has not been informed.

THE SEED OF ABRAHAM

Later, the Lord appeared to Abraham again to reaffirm and elaborate on His promises. This time, Abraham asked how he would inherit the promises, since he didn't even have a son. What happened next is pure poetry. The Lord took Abraham outside beneath the night sky and said, "Now look toward the heavens, and count the stars, if you are able to count them. So shall your descendants be" (Gen 15:5). In Abraham's day, without light pollution, the night sky would have been radiant with stars—a powerful visual aid. The Lord used this magical moment to assure Abraham that not only would he have a son, but his descendants would be innumerable: "One who will come forth from your own body, he shall be your heir" (Gen 15:4).

At first glance, this appears to be a simple promise of many descendants. But the promise is more nuanced. While Abraham eventually had eight sons (Gen 25), the covenant promises were only made to the descendants of Isaac (Gen 21:12; 17:15–21), and then to Isaac's son Jacob (Gen 28:13–14), whose name was later changed to Israel (Gen 32:28).

Yet the promise narrows even further. Ultimately, the promises would be fulfilled through one specific individual, one particular *seed* from the family of Israel. Many centuries later, the Apostle Paul would clarify: "Now the promises were spoken to Abraham and to his seed. He does not say, 'And to seeds,' as one would in referring to many, but rather as in referring to one, 'And to your seed,' that is, Christ" (Gal 3:16).

ABRAHAM THE BELIEVER

We must pay close attention to what comes next. At this very moment, Scripture says:

"Abraham believed the Lord, and He counted it to him as righteousness" (Genesis 15:6).

What exactly did Abraham believe that led him to be deemed as righteous?

Correctly understanding this is critical. Abraham was not considered righteous by God for merely believing that God would give him a son. Abraham had a well-developed understanding of the Promised One and the Lord's plan of redemption. Ever since the declaration in Eden, the righteous had been looking forward to the Redeemer. Abraham understood that the *seed* promised to him was the same *seed* promised to Eve. He knew this *seed* would inherit the land, crush the serpent, and bless the nations. Abraham did not know about the cross, but he understood that the Promised One would suffer, yet emerge victorious. He knew this *seed* would reverse the curse. Abraham's understanding of the Gospel, though less detailed than ours today, was robust. Upon hearing these promises, he placed his trust in God and fixed his hope in the *seed*. This is why Jesus said: "Your father Abraham rejoiced to see My day, and he saw it and was glad" (John 8:56). And as Paul wrote: "God preached the gospel beforehand to Abraham" (Gal 3:8). Paul is clear that the essence of the gospel message was announced to Abraham in advance. While Abraham's understanding was not as advanced as ours, his faith was just as genuine and profound. He was counted righteous because he trusted God and placed his hope in the coming Redeemer. Paul affirms this in Romans 4 and Galatians 3:7: "Be sure that it is those who are of faith who are sons of Abraham."

THE COVENANT BETWEEN THE PARTS

To seal His promises, God enacted a formal covenant ceremony. Abraham was instructed to bring a heifer, a goat, a ram, a turtledove, and a pigeon (Gen 15:9), then cut them in two and lay the pieces opposite each other. As Abraham slept, God appeared as a smoking firepot and a flaming torch, passing between the pieces (Gen 15:17).

THE ABRAHAMIC COVENANT

Jews call this the *Berit bein HaBetarim*—"The Covenant Between the Parts." By walking between the slain animals, God was making a solemn oath, essentially saying: "If I break my promise, may I become like these dead animals."

There is also another significant prophetic revelation within the story of the covenant. As the Lord was about to execute the covenant and bestow upon Abraham and his descendants their high calling, Abraham was shown the future of his people. When he saw this, we are told that the "horror of great darkness fell upon him" (Gen 15:12). What exactly did Abraham see? Was it merely the 400 years of enslavement in Egypt, or did he see all of Israel's painful history? Did he see so far into the future that he caught a glimpse of the Holocaust itself? Extraordinary callings always come with a great price. Surely, if any people in the world have carried the highest of all callings and paid the heaviest and most horrific price, it has been the Jewish people. But their story is far from over.

THE SEED WHO WILL BE PROVIDED

Among all of Abraham's experiences, none reveals God's redemptive plan more clearly than the binding of Isaac in Genesis 22. This was not just a test of obedience—it was a prophecy.

God had promised a son. That son had come. And now, without explanation, God commanded:

"Take now your son, your only son, whom you love, Isaac, and go...
and offer him there as a burnt offering" (Genesis 22:2).

Unthinkable. Yet Abraham obeyed. Rising early, he journeyed to Mount Moriah, carrying fire, wood, and a knife. On the way, Isaac asked one of the most poignant questions in Scripture: "Behold, the fire and the wood, but where is the lamb for the burnt offering?" And Abraham, with prophetic insight, replied:

"God will provide for Himself the lamb for the burnt offering, my son" (Genesis 22:7–8).

Abraham had been told that the covenant *seed* would come through Isaac (Gen 21:12). He believed that even if Isaac died, God would raise him from the dead (Heb 11:19). He believed in resurrection because he believed God's promise. At the altar, as the knife was raised, the angel of the Lord stopped him:

"Do not stretch out your hand against the lad..." (Genesis 22:12).

A ram was caught in the thicket—but it was not a lamb. Abraham named the place *YHVH Yireh*—"The Lord Will Provide." Notice: he didn't say *the Lord has provided*. Abraham knew the real Lamb was still to come.

Moses later recorded this forward-looking promise:

"As it is said to this day, 'On the mount of the Lord, it will be provided'" (Genesis 22:14).

Both Abraham and Moses were looking ahead to a day when God would provide His Lamb on that very mountain in Jerusalem.

Then the Lord reaffirmed His promise with powerful words:

"By Myself I have sworn... I will greatly bless you... And your seed shall possess the gate of His enemies. In your seed all the nations of the earth shall be blessed" (Genesis 22:16–18).

This is Skull Crusher language. The *seed* will triumph over His enemies. He will conquer. He will reign.

THE LORD WILL PROVIDE THE LAMB

REITERATION AND EXPANSION OF THE COVENANT

Throughout the Scriptures, God repeats and expands the covenant—first to Abraham (Gen 15, 17, 18, 22), then to Isaac (Gen 26:3–4), and finally to Jacob (Gen 27:29; 28:13–14).

One moment with Jacob stands out. As Isaac unknowingly blessed Jacob instead of Esau, he prophesied:

> "May peoples serve you, And nations bow down to you; Be master of your brothers... Cursed be those who curse you, And blessed be those who bless you" (Genesis 27:29).

Many believe the Abrahamic Covenant is simply about the land. It is, but inherent in the promise of the land is the promise of kingship. Here, it is made explicit: the promised seed will rule over many peoples and nations. He will be a great king to whom the world will bow. Those who honor Him will be blessed.

CONCLUSION

Now we are beginning to see the beautiful golden thread of messianic expectation that is woven throughout the Bible. Here in the life of Abraham, the seed of hope planted in the garden has already sprouted up and begun to grow.

The seed of Eve is also the seed of Abraham, who would come through the line of Isaac and Jacob. It is from the chosen line of Israel that the Promised One would come. He will inherit the promised land, rule as king, and free the world from the corruption introduced by Satan, thus bringing the Lord's unrestrained blessings to the whole earth. The Lord sealed His promises through a blood covenant. It was upon His very own life that He made this most solemn oath. As we follow the thread of messianic hope throughout the Scriptures, before we even complete the Book of Genesis, the Lord's promised plan of redemption is already very well defined.

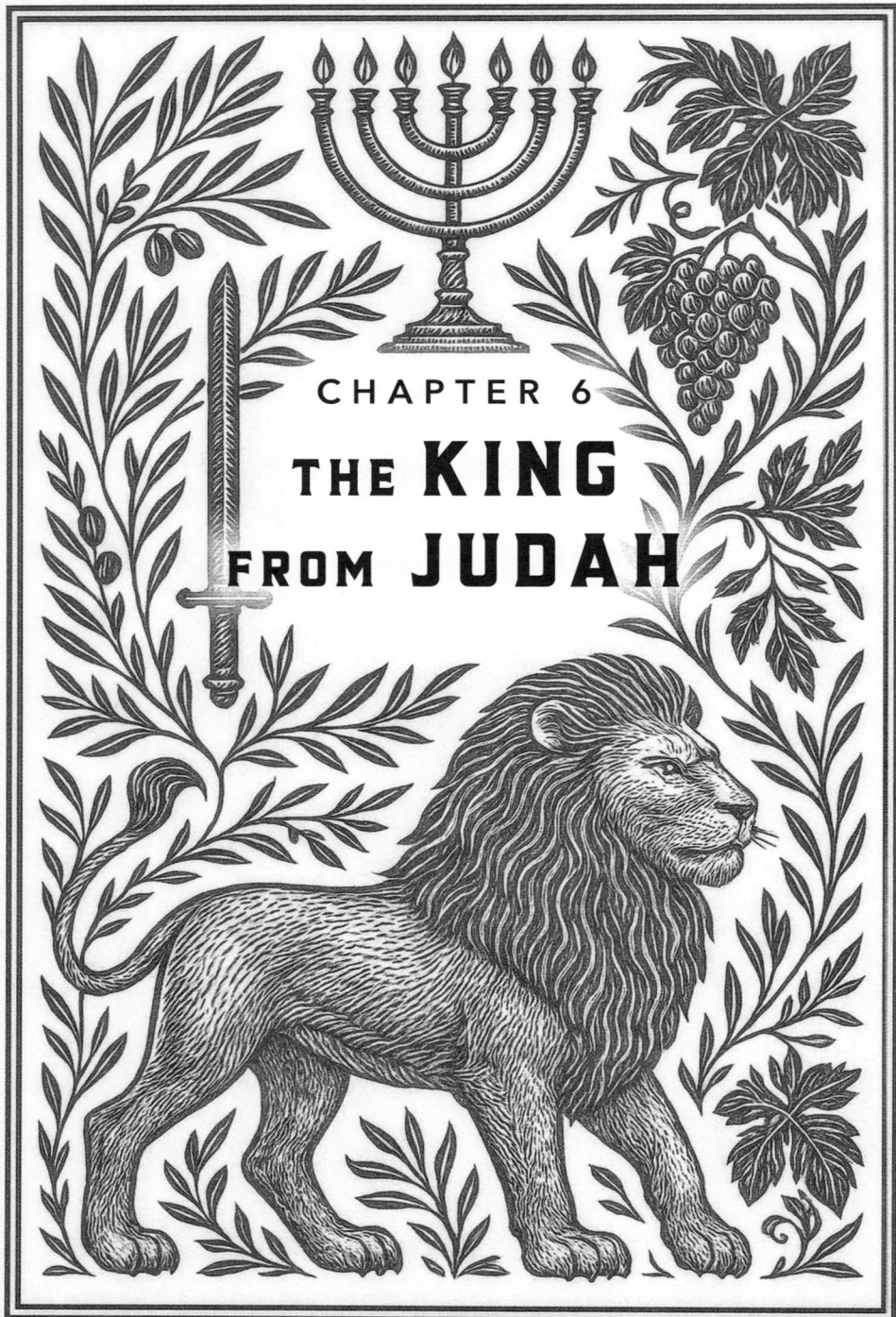

CHAPTER 6

THE KING
FROM JUDAH

WHEN ABRAHAM'S GRANDSON JACOB reached the age of 147, he knew his death was near. As his final act, he gathered his twelve sons to bless, judge, and prophesy over each one:

> "Then Jacob summoned his sons and said, 'Assemble yourselves that I may tell you what will befall you in the days to come. Gather together and hear, O sons of Jacob; and listen to Israel your father'" (Genesis 49:1–2).

The words "gather" and "hear" mark the solemn and prophetic nature of what Jacob was about to speak. The phrase "in the days to come" reveals that his words looked beyond the lives of his immediate sons—they were prophetic words concerning the destinies of their descendants, even stretching into the last days.

THE BLESSING OF JUDAH

While the longest of Jacob's twelve blessings was given to Joseph, the most significant and messianic prophecy was spoken over Judah. In Jacob's words, we find the next great revelation concerning the promised deliverer:

> "Judah, your brothers shall praise you; Your hand shall be on the neck of your enemies; Your father's sons shall bow down to you" (Genesis 49:8).

This verse contains three distinct and prophetic declarations: First, Judah will be praised by his brothers—remarkable, since praise in Scripture is nearly always reserved for God alone. That the one who comes from Judah receives praise hints at His divine identity. Second, he will subdue his enemies—echoing the earlier promise of the One who would crush the serpent. Third, his brothers will bow before him—a clear nod to royal authority and future kingship.

It's as though Jacob, having long wondered which of his sons would

JACOB'S PROPHECY TO JUDAH

carry the line of the Promised One, finally proclaims with joy, "Judah, you are the one."

THE LION OF JUDAH

Jacob continues with one of the most iconic and powerful images in all of messianic prophecy:

"Judah is a lion's whelp; From the prey, my son, you have gone up. He couches, he lies down as a lion, And as a lion, who dares rouse him?" (Genesis 49:9).

The image is that of a lion—victorious in battle—resting after the hunt. It is from this verse that the Book of Revelation later describes Jesus as "the Lion of the tribe of Judah" (Rev 5:5). This New Testament affirmation confirms the messianic and end-time nature of Jacob's blessing. It is not merely about Judah, but about the One who would rise from his line—Jesus, the conquering King.

THE KING FROM JUDAH

The prophecy continues with a bold declaration of kingship:

"The scepter shall not depart from Judah, Nor the ruler's staff from between his feet, Until Shiloh comes, And to him shall be the obedience of the peoples" (Genesis 49:10).

The phrase "between his feet" is a poetic way of referring to one's offspring or "seed." In this context, it suggests a royal lineage that will arise from Judah and endure.

The expression "until Shiloh comes" has been interpreted in several ways. Some see "Shiloh" as a proper name for the Messiah. Others interpret it to mean "until tribute comes to him," or "Until he to whom it belongs comes."

All of these interpretations point in the same direction: a ruler will

THE LION OF JUDAH

come from Judah, and when He arrives, the obedience of all nations will belong to Him. The scope is global. This is no mere tribal leader—this is the King of kings.

HE WASHES HIS GARMENTS IN WINE

Jacob's prophecy continues with a rich, though somewhat cryptic, poetic flourish:

> "He ties his foal to the vine, And his donkey's colt to the choice vine;
> He washes his garments in wine, And his robes in the blood of grapes.
> His eyes are dull from wine, And his teeth white from milk" (Genesis 49:11–12).

Christian and Jewish interpreters have long debated the meaning of these verses. Some Christians have tried to find detailed connections to Jesus' earthly ministry—for example, interpreting the tied colt as a foreshadowing of His triumphal entry into Jerusalem. Martin Luther even suggested the foal symbolized the Church, intoxicated with the Holy Spirit.

Jewish interpretations, though rejecting New Testament fulfillment, still affirm the messianic nature of the prophecy. The *Legends of the Jews*, a classic compilation of Jewish traditions, paraphrases Jacob's message like this:

> "No people and no kingdom will be able to stand up against thee. Rulers shall not cease from the house of Judah, nor teachers of the law from his posterity, until his descendant Messiah come, and the obedience of all peoples be unto him. How glorious is Messiah of the House of Judah! His loins girded, he will go out to do battle with his enemies. No king and no ruler will prevail against him. The mountains will be dyed red with their blood, and the garments of Messiah will be like the garments of him that presseth wine."

The prophet Isaiah draws from this same imagery, describing the coming warrior-king whose garments are stained from treading the winepress (Isa 63:1–6). We'll explore Isaiah's prophecy later, but the connection is clear: Jacob foresaw not only kingship, but judgment and bloodshed of a warrior, reminiscent of the serpent-crushing Seed.

At the same time, some details of the prophecy may also describe the physical land given to Judah, especially its abundance of vineyards and pastures. Wine and milk are biblical symbols of blessing and prosperity (cf. Isa 55:1). Like many biblical prophecies, the passage blends the earthly and the eschatological, the immediate and the ultimate.

JACOB'S FINAL MOMENTS

Genesis 49 closes with a personal and touching glimpse into Jacob's final moments:

> "When Jacob finished charging his sons, he drew his feet into the bed and breathed his last, and was gathered to his people" (Genesis 49:33).

The blessing of Judah, however, remains as one of the brightest lights in the unfolding messianic story. We now see the golden thread more clearly than ever: the *seed of the woman* is also the *seed of Abraham*, and now He is revealed as the *king from the tribe of Judah*.

This King will receive universal praise, defeat His enemies, and command the obedience of all nations. The Lion of Judah will reign forever.

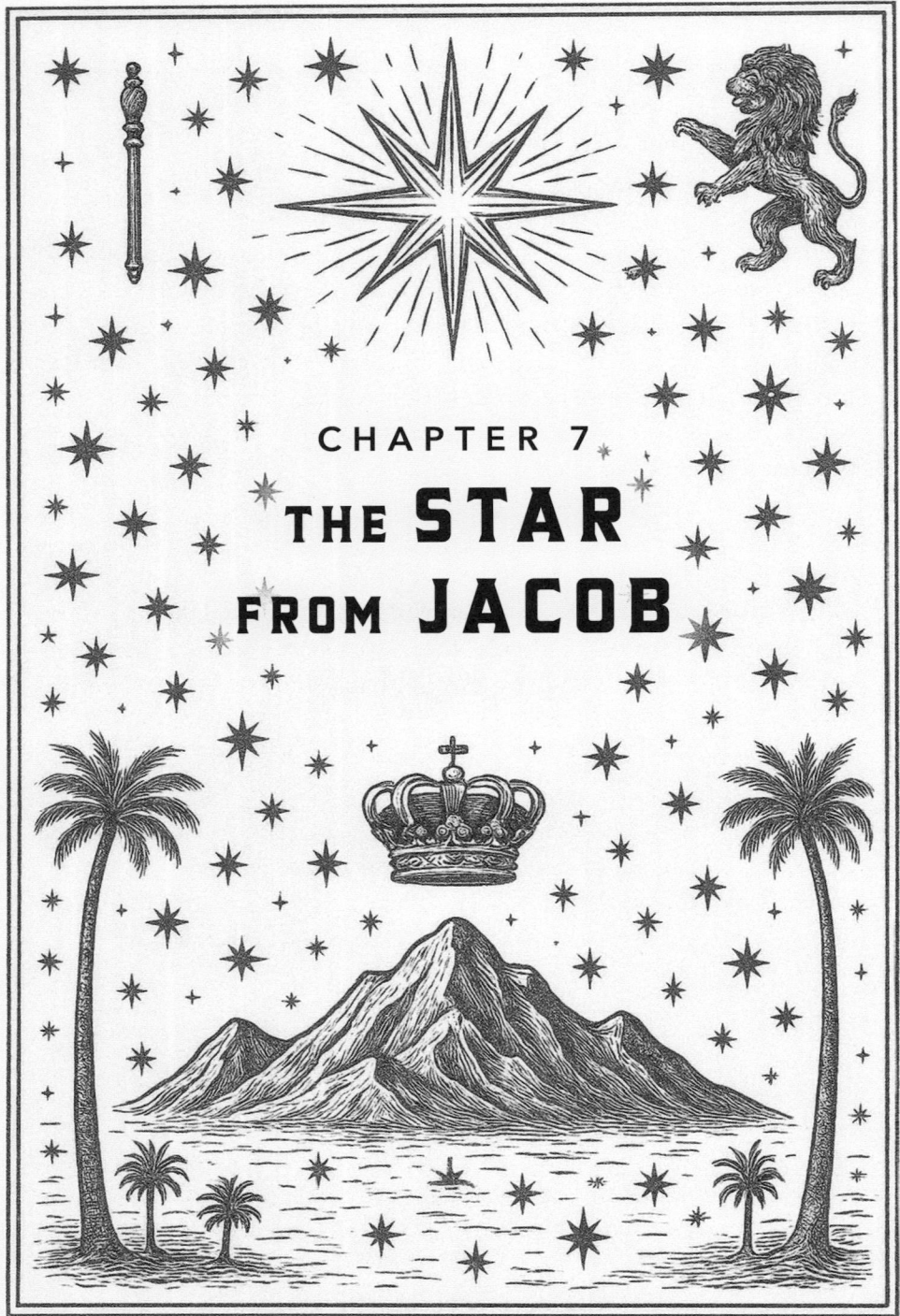

CHAPTER 7

THE **STAR** FROM **JACOB**

CONTINUING TO FOLLOW THE GOLDEN THREAD of God's promise-plan, we come to the prophecies of Balaam—one of the most enigmatic figures in the Bible. Balaam was the son of Beor, from Pethor, a city near the Euphrates River in Mesopotamia (Num 22:5), close to where modern-day Turkey, Syria, and Iraq converge. Though Balaam was essentially a diviner—a spiritual mercenary for hire—the Lord chose to speak through him powerfully. Despite his corrupt character, Balaam delivered some of the most foundational messianic prophecies in all of Scripture. His oracles are rich, poetic, and deeply prophetic, foretelling a future King from Israel who would conquer God's enemies and rule the nations. These words build upon Jacob's blessing to Judah and become the next knot on the golden thread of Israel's messianic hope.

ISRAEL NEARS THE LAND

At this point, Israel had arrived at the plains of Moab, just east of the Jordan River, directly across from Jericho. Having defeated the Amorites and the giant clans of Bashan (Num 21), Israel's military victories struck fear into the surrounding nations. Balak, king of Moab, alarmed by Israel's encroachment upon his territory, sought supernatural help. He summoned Balaam, a well-known seer from distant Pethor. Balak pleaded, "Come now, curse this people for me... for I know that he whom you bless is blessed, and he whom you curse is cursed" (Num 22:6). But in a twist of divine irony, God placed His own words in Balaam's mouth. No matter how many times Balak tried to manipulate him into pronouncing a curse, Balaam could only bless Israel.

THE DONKEY AND THE ANGEL

When Balaam agreed to go with Balak's messengers, the Lord was angered, for Balaam's heart was set on unrighteous gain. So the Lord sent an angel to confront him on the road. Strangely, Balaam was blind to the angel's presence, while his donkey saw the divine messenger and refused to move forward. Enraged, Balaam beat the poor animal—until the Lord opened her mouth and she asked: "What have I done to you, that you have struck me these three times?" (Num 22:28). Then, God opened Balaam's eyes, and he too saw the angel standing before him. The Bible doesn't say the donkey was suddenly given intelligence—only that her mouth was opened. Yet she spoke a simple, cogent question: "What have I done?" Her plaintive words, her years of faithful service seem to carry a note of grief: "Am I not your donkey, on which you have ridden all your life to this day? Have I ever acted this way before?" To which Balaam sheepishly answered, "No" (Num 22:30). The lesson is clear: Balaam, the supposed seer, was blind to God's presence. His donkey, by contrast, saw what he could not. This sets the stage for what follows, in which God will use another unlikely vessel—Balaam himself. When God speaks, His word will be heard, even through a donkey or a greedy sorcerer.

BALAAM'S FIRST ORACLE

Balak took Balaam to several high places overlooking Israel's encampment, hoping one of them might serve as a vantage point for cursing the people. But instead, the Spirit of God came upon Balaam, and blessings poured from his lips:

> "How fair are your tents, O Jacob, Your dwellings, O Israel! Like valleys that stretch out, Like gardens beside the river, Like aloes planted by the Lord, Like cedars beside the waters" (Numbers 24:5–6).

These poetic lines speak only of divine favor and flourishing. Then the prophecy shifts toward Israel's future King:

> "Water will flow from his buckets, And his seed will be by many waters, And his king shall be higher than Agag, And his kingdom shall be exalted" (v. 7).

What does it mean that Israel's king will be "higher than Agag"? Agag was the king of Amalek during King Saul's time—a few centuries

BALAAM

after Balaam's day. Many scholars believe "Agag" here may be a textual corruption. Several ancient versions—including the Septuagint, the Samaritan Pentateuch, Aquila, Theodotion, and Symmachus—read "Gog" instead. This would make Balaam's oracle the earliest biblical reference to Gog, the future enemy of God's people, later described in the famous prophecy of Ezekiel 38–39. Balaam's prophecy would then pit Israel's exalted Seed and King against Gog—the ultimate embodiment of the seed of the serpent.

THE WILD OX AND THE LION

The prophecy continues:

> "God brings him out of Egypt... He is for him like the horns of the wild ox. He will devour the nations who are his adversaries, And will crush their bones in pieces, And shatter them with his arrows" (v. 8).

Here, the messianic theme of Skull Crusher resurfaces. This King will not only crush Satan, but also all who align with him. God's enemies are Israel's enemies, and His victory is Israel's. Balaam ends this oracle by echoing the blessings first given to Abraham and later to Judah:

> "He couches, he lies down as a lion, And as a lion, who dares rouse him? Blessed is everyone who blesses you, And cursed is everyone who curses you" (v. 9).

The King cannot be separated from His people. The dominion and blessing promised to Israel belong to her Messiah. To bless Him is to bless them; to curse Him is to curse them.

BALAAM'S SECOND ORACLE

Though enraged by Balaam's words, Balak persisted. Balaam, however, stood firm: "I can only speak what the Lord gives me." Then came another one of the most foundational messianic prophecies in all of Scripture:

"I see him, but not now; I behold him, but not near; A star shall come forth from Jacob, A scepter shall rise from Israel, And shall crush through the forehead of Moab, And tear down all the sons of Sheth" (v. 17).

The imagery is explicit: the star and scepter speak of royalty. This is Israel's King, destined to arise. He will crush Moab's forehead—echoing Genesis 3:15. The "sons of Sheth" likely represent violent enemies of God. Though David waged war against these people, he never fully defeated them. The complete conquest will be reserved for a far greater King—Jesus the Messiah.

This prophecy opens with the vision of the Messiah's appearance and ends with the downfall of the Antichrist. It is a sweeping glimpse of history's climax.

Balaam continues: "One from Jacob shall have dominion, and will destroy the remnant from the city." (v. 19). This is not a mere localized ruler; this is a global King who will subdue all nations.

A PROPHETIC BLUEPRINT

There is beautiful irony in the fact that one of the most exalted messianic prophecies came through a greedy seer-for-hire. Balaam meant it for profit. Balak meant it for harm. But God meant it for His own glory.

The intended curse became a blessing. The plan to stop Israel became a declaration of her destiny.

Centuries later, magi from the east followed a star in search of the newborn King (Matt 2:2). Many scholars believe these men were heirs to eastern prophetic traditions—possibly even influenced by Balaam's legacy. If so, then Balaam not only foresaw the Messiah but also helped initiate the first Gentile response to His arrival.

CONCLUSION

Balaam saw Him, though distant in time, he saw the One who would rise from the house of Jacob. He saw the Star, the Scepter, the Skull

HE WILL CRUSH THE FOREHEAD OF MOAB

Crusher, and the Ruler of nations.

Balaam's prophecies are another brilliant node on the golden thread of God's promises. Today, we can say that while the star has risen, the scepter is still to come. The day is drawing closer to that incandescent age when all nations will all bow before the star and the scepter—the King of Israel.

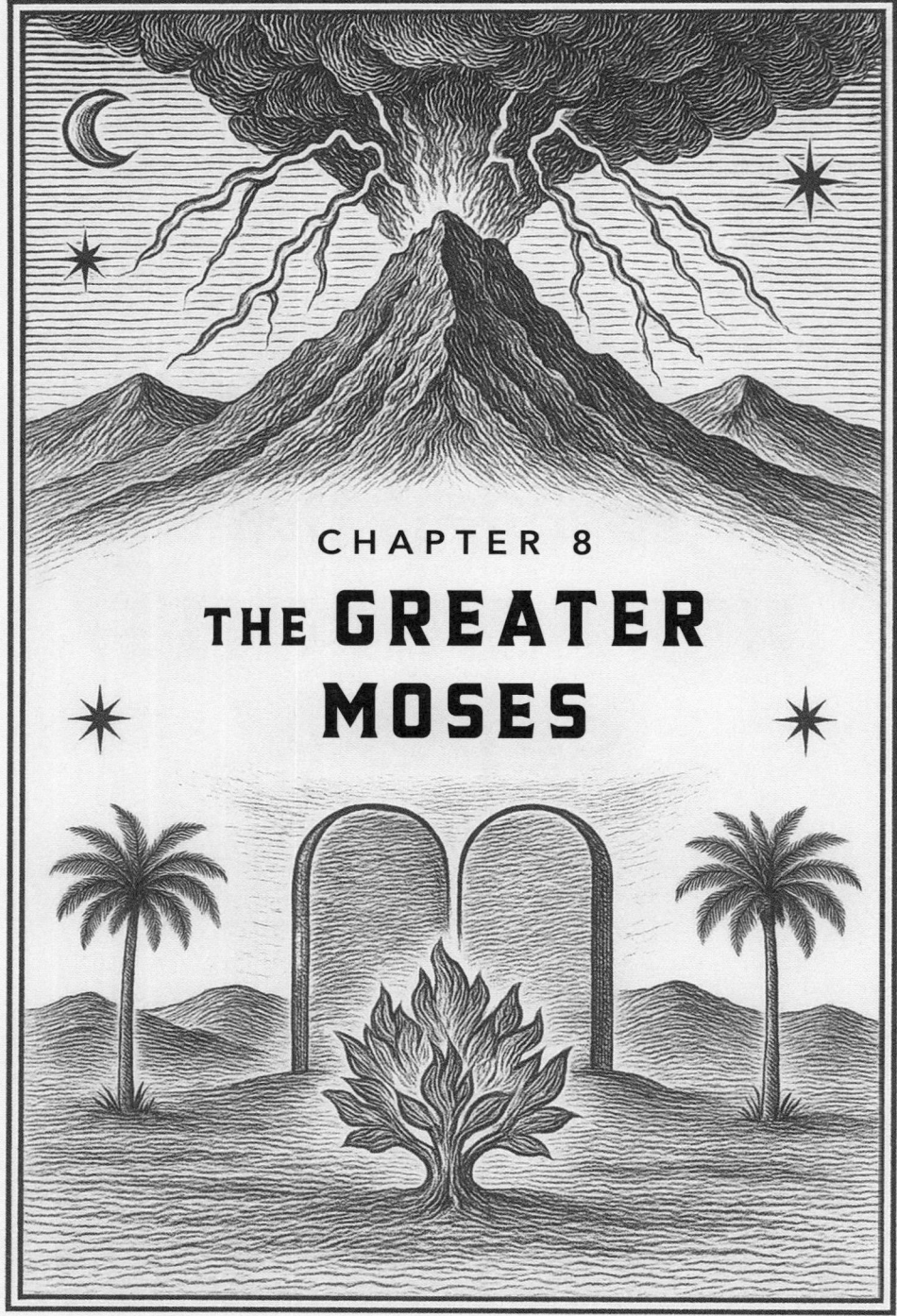

CHAPTER 8

THE **GREATER** MOSES

AS ISRAEL'S TIME OF WANDERING in the desert drew to a close, Moses stood before the nation and looked to the future. The promised land lay just beyond the Jordan, but Moses himself would not enter it. His death was near. Before his departure, the Lord gave him a final series of specific instructions—reminders, warnings, and prophetic glimpses of what was yet to come. Among these was a particularly profound promise concerning the future of divine leadership in Israel: the Lord would raise up a prophet.

The passage in question is found in Deuteronomy 18. After condemning the occult practices of the Canaanite nations—witchcraft, divination, necromancy—the Lord declared that His people were not to seek guidance through such dark and deceptive means. Yet God did not leave His people without a means to hear from Him. Instead, He made a stunning promise:

> "The Lord your God will raise up for you a prophet like me from among you, from your countrymen—you shall listen to him. This is according to all that you asked of the Lord your God in Horeb on the day of the assembly, saying, 'Let me not hear again the voice of the Lord my God, let me not see this great fire anymore, or I will die.' The Lord said to me, 'They have spoken well. I will raise up a prophet from among their countrymen like you, and I will put My words in his mouth, and he shall speak to them all that I command him'" (Deuteronomy 18:15-18).

This prophecy stands as one of the most significant messianic promises in the Torah. It contains both a near-term and a long-term fulfillment. On the one hand, it speaks of a line of prophets who would carry the divine message to Israel after Moses. On the other hand, it points forward to the coming of a singular, extraordinary Prophet—one who would not only be like Moses but would surpass him.

PROPHETS LIKE MOSES—AND THE ONE WHO IS GREATER

To understand this promise, we must remember the context. At Mount Sinai, when God had first spoken directly to the people, they were overwhelmed. They begged for a mediator—for someone who would stand between them and God. Moses became that mediator, and the prophetic office was born. From now on, the Lord would raise up prophets to speak His words on His behalf.

These prophets would have to meet specific qualifications. First, they had to be Israelites—"from among your countrymen." This immediately excludes later foreign claimants, such as Muhammad, who was not from Israel and thus cannot fulfill this prophecy, despite frequent assertions of Muslims to the contrary.

Second, the prophet must be "like Moses." What does this mean? It certainly includes a level of intimacy with God. Moses was not merely a prophet—he was the mediator of a covenant, the deliverer of Israel, the one through whom the Lord revealed His Law. He spoke to God "face to face, just as a man speaks to his friend" (Ex 33:11). No prophet in Israel's history matched the uniqueness of Moses. Deuteronomy 34:10 explicitly affirms this: "Since that time no prophet has risen in Israel like Moses, whom the Lord knew face to face."

Though Elijah, Elisha, Isaiah, and Jeremiah were mighty messengers of God, none stood on equal footing with Moses. They all looked forward to someone far greater. And so, while Deuteronomy 18 indeed affirmed the coming prophetic tradition in Israel, it also anticipated the arrival of *the* Prophet—someone who would fulfill the role in a way no one else could.

THE MESSIAH AS THE PROPHET LIKE MOSES

There are compelling reasons to see Deuteronomy 18 as ultimately pointing to the Messiah.

First, the text refers to "a prophet," not a group. Although the broader passage acknowledges many prophets, this specific prophecy focuses on one figure: "you shall listen to *him*." This singular focus is reinforced later by Peter and Stephen in the book of Acts, who both apply this prophecy directly to Jesus (Acts 3:22; 7:37).

This expectation also surfaces repeatedly in the Gospels. When John the Baptist began his ministry, the religious leaders asked him plainly, "Are you the Prophet?" (Jn 1:21). After Jesus miraculously fed the five thousand, the people exclaimed, "This is truly the Prophet who is to come into the world" (Jn 6:14). Others said, "This certainly is the Prophet," while still others said, "This is the Christ" (Jn 7:40–41). Some believed these were two distinct figures; others rightly saw them as the same.

Second, the prophet must be "like Moses." Yet Deuteronomy itself testifies that no prophet in Israel's history rose to that level. "Since that time no prophet has risen in Israel like Moses, whom the Lord knew face to face" (Deut 34:10). Moses was not merely a messenger—he was the covenant mediator, the lawgiver, the deliverer of Israel, and the friend of God.

Only Jesus fulfills and surpasses this description. Like Moses, He delivers His people, but from sin and death rather than Pharaoh. Like Moses, He mediates a covenant—but a new and better one, written not on tablets of stone but on hearts of flesh (Heb 8:6–10). And while Moses climbed Mount Sinai to receive the word of God, Jesus came down from heaven as the Word of God made flesh (Jn 1:14).

In the Sermon on the Mount, Jesus didn't merely echo Moses—He spoke with divine authority: "You have heard that it was said... but I say to you" (Matt 5:21–48). He did not just speak *for* God—He spoke *as* God. "I and the Father are one," He declared (Jn 10:30).

JESUS: PROPHET, PRIEST, AND KING

Jesus is not merely "like" Moses; He is greater. As the book of Hebrews declares:

> "For He has been counted worthy of more glory than Moses, by just so much as the builder of the house has more honor than the house" (Hebrews 3:3).

MOSES AND JESUS

Moses was a faithful servant in God's house. Jesus is the Son over it (Heb 3:5–6). Moses pointed forward to something greater. Jesus is the fulfillment of that hope.

He is the Prophet who speaks God's words because He *is* the Word. He is the mediator of the New Covenant, the one whose blood brings eternal redemption. He is our Great High Priest who has passed through the heavens (Heb 4:14). And He is the promised King—the King of kings and Lord of lords (Rev 19:16).

In Jesus, all the hopes and roles anticipated in the Old Testament find their culmination.

CONCLUSION

Deuteronomy 18 is an instruction about prophets, but also contains a messianic prophecy. While it affirms the prophetic office for Israel's future, it also sets the stage for the arrival of one extraordinary Prophet—an individual who would be like Moses, yet far greater.

That Prophet is Jesus of Nazareth. He is the greater Moses, the mediator of the New Covenant, and the one who leads His people, not just into a land of promise, but into the Kingdom of God itself, the ultimate *Promised Land*.

As Peter declared to the people of Jerusalem:

> "Moses said, 'The Lord God will raise up for you a prophet like me from your brethren; to him you shall give heed in everything He says to you.' … And likewise, all the prophets who have spoken, from Samuel and his successors onward, also announced these days" (Acts 3:22, 24).

The wait is over. The Prophet, greater than Moses, has come. Let us listen to Him.

THE PROPHET GREATER THAN MOSES

CHAPTER 9

THE CLOUD RIDER

LONG BEFORE MOSES, the ancient patriarch Enoch, a mere seven generations from Adam, delivered one of the most stunning descriptions of the Lord's coming in the last days. His words were preserved and later quoted in the New Testament. We cite them here as they appear in the book of Jude:

> "Behold, the Lord came with many thousands of His holy ones, to execute judgment upon all, and to convict all the ungodly of all their ungodly deeds..." (Jude 14–15)

This ancient vision portrays the Lord coming from heaven with "myriads of His holy ones," not to comfort the nations, but to confront them—to judge the wicked and save the righteous.

Much later, at the conclusion of Israel's time wandering in the desert, just before he died, Moses gathered the leaders of the tribes of Israel, and like Jacob before him, he began to prophesy over each tribe. His prophecy is stunningly similar to that which Enoch had prophesied generations earlier, but Moses fills in many details that Enoch passed over. The prophecy begins with a glorious description of YHVH coming from heaven, marching forward from the land of Sinai, shining like the morning sun and accompanied by an army of angels:

> "The Lord came from Sinai, and dawned on them from Seir; He shone forth from Mount Paran, And He came from the midst of ten thousand holy ones; At His right hand there was flashing lightning for them." (Deuteronomy 33:2)

Throughout the entire Torah, this is one of the most foundational yet widely misunderstood verses. Far more than a poetic look back at the dramatic events of Mount Sinai, Deuteronomy 33:2 is a prophetic glimpse of the future—a vision of the Lord God Almighty coming from heaven to deliver His people. The vision does not stop with verse 2.

THE BLESSING OF MOSES

THE KING IN JESHURUN

A few verses later, we find another critical line:

> "He became king in Jeshurun, when the heads of the people were gathered, the tribes of Israel together." (Deuteronomy 33:5)

Jeshurun is a poetic name for Israel, meaning "my upright ones." Here, Moses sees God reigning as King when the people are all gathered and united.

After the majestic One comes from heaven, He is enthroned in the midst of His gathered tribes. This passage specifically anticipates a future time of regathering when Israel will be united with God as King in their midst. He will not reign from heaven above but from the earth below, present among His people.

THE CLOUD RIDER

As the prophecy concludes, verses 26–27 expand the vision even more:

> "There is no one like the God of Jeshurun, who rides across the heavens to help you and on the clouds in his majesty. The eternal God is your refuge, and underneath are the everlasting arms. He will drive out your enemies before you, saying, 'Destroy them!'" (Deuteronomy 33:26–27)

The language here could not be more explicit. Among all the gods of the earth, there is no one like YHVH, "the God of Jeshurun," the One who rides across the heavens on the clouds to save His beloved people. YHVH is the only true Cloud Rider. He does not quietly float down on the clouds; He comes in overwhelming, terrifying majesty. His arrival brings salvation for His people and the judgment and destruction of His enemies. The arms that uphold His people are the same arms that will cast down their oppressors. Verse 26 shows us that God's coming will be majestic, cosmic, and visible to all. Verse 27 also reveals His personal,

THE CLOUD RIDER

tender presence—He is a shelter, a refuge, and a firm and everlasting foundation that ever supports His people.

Moses is declaring that the same God who once descended upon Sinai in fire and cloud will come again, riding through the skies, coming on the clouds, blazing with glory, and leading legions of holy ones. This is the foundation upon which the later prophets and apostles built their visions of the Lord's return. It is the origin of what we may call the prophecies of the Cloud Rider.

SINAI TO ZION: A JOURNEY YET TO BE COMPLETED

Moses speaks of the Lord coming from Sinai, then from Seir, then from Mount Paran. These are not mythical locations. They are literal places in the deserts to the southeast of Israel. Mount Sinai, of course, is the mountain of the covenant. Today, the real Mount Sinai is located in northwestern Saudi Arabia. Mount Seir was the chief mountain in the Kingdom of Edom. Today, this correlates to Petra in the Kingdom of Jordan. Mount Paran lies in the northern reaches of the Arabian wilderness. It is the tallest mountain in the Kingdom of Jordan, located on the border with Saudi Arabia, and is known in Arabic as *Jebel Umm ad-Dami*. I've had the pleasure of not only seeing but also climbing these mountains. Moses did not outline some random path; it is an intentional route—one that traces the Lord's coming march through the desert when He returns. Unlike the exodus generation wandering around the desert, here the movement is direct and purposeful. It is the Lord God Almighty Himself marching through the desert.

THE RETURN OF JESUS

This journey is yet to be completed. While the Lord once led Israel through the deserts of the Exodus in the form of the pillar of cloud, there remains a greater exodus, another march through the wilderness, through which He will save His people, judge the nations, and ultimately, establish His throne in Zion. Moses' vision portrays God as the ultimate Divine Warrior. After Israel had fled through the Red Sea, after experiencing such an unfathomably miraculous deliverance, they stood on the shore of the sea and sang a song of worshipful celebration. There they declared, "YHVH is a warrior; YHVH is His name." (Ex 15:3). The similarities between this passage and Enoch's prophecy are also undeniable. The logical conclusion is stunning. This majestic description of YHVH, the Lord God Almighty, coming from heaven, with lightning in His hand, is a vision of the return of Jesus. He comes surrounded by "ten thousand holy ones"—a phrase later echoed by Jesus Himself when He described His return.

THE SECOND EXODUS

One of the most striking themes in the prophets is the repeated promise that the Lord will gather His people once again in a second Exodus. Isaiah 11:15–16 says the Lord will dry up the Egyptian sea and make a highway for the remnant of His people, just as He did when they came up from Egypt. Ezekiel 20:35–38 describes the Lord bringing Israel into "the wilderness of the peoples" to confront them face to face, to purge the rebels, and to bring the remnant into covenant relationship. But this time, the one leading the exodus is not Moses. It is God Himself, the Cloud Rider, followed by an army of angels.

WHO IS THE CLOUD RIDER?

The title "Cloud Rider" has a fascinating backstory. In ancient Near Eastern mythology, as depicted in the Ugaritic text known as "The Baal Cycle," Baal was not only recognized as the storm god, but he was specifically referred to as "the one who rides upon the clouds." The biblical prophets deliberately co-opted this title, declaring that it is YHVH alone who truly rides the clouds. Psalm 68:4 proclaims, "Sing to God, sing praises to His name; lift up a song for Him who rides on the clouds, whose name is the Lord."

This imagery also appears in the prophetic vision of Isaiah: "Behold, the Lord is riding on a swift cloud and is about to come to Egypt; the idols of Egypt will tremble at His presence" (Isaiah 19:1). In all these

WITH MYRIADS OF HIS HOLY ONES

scenes, it is God—not Baal, not any lesser being—who is seated above the heavens and coming in fire and fury.

THE ROAD TO ZION

The message of Deuteronomy 33 is unmistakable: Israel's journey from Sinai to Zion is not yet complete. The first exodus lies behind us, but the second exodus still lies ahead. The same God who once descended upon Sinai in fire and cloud will come again—and will follow the same path through the wilderness. The One who once led Israel through the desert as a pillar of cloud will return, not in mystery or symbol, but in unveiled glory.

This is not the rapture of the Church to heaven. This is heaven's King coming down. It is an invasion. A hostile takeover. The return of the Lord in power, splendor, and fire.

The God of Sinai will once again ride upon the clouds. He will shatter the rebellious among the nations, redeem His people, and establish His throne in Zion. His march through the desert will not be a wandering, but a procession of victory. He will come as the Divine Warrior, blazing in majesty, accompanied by tens of thousands of holy ones.

The visions of Enoch and Moses form the foundation for all later prophetic expectation. This is the hope of the prophets. This is the longing of the apostles. This is the destiny declared from the earliest pages of Scripture: the Cloud Rider is coming.

This is the ultimate fulfillment of the promise—the Seed of the woman, the Seed of Abraham, the Lion of Judah, the King from Jacob—coming again in the clouds to crush the serpent and take back the earth.

This is our hope. *Come, Lord Jesus.*

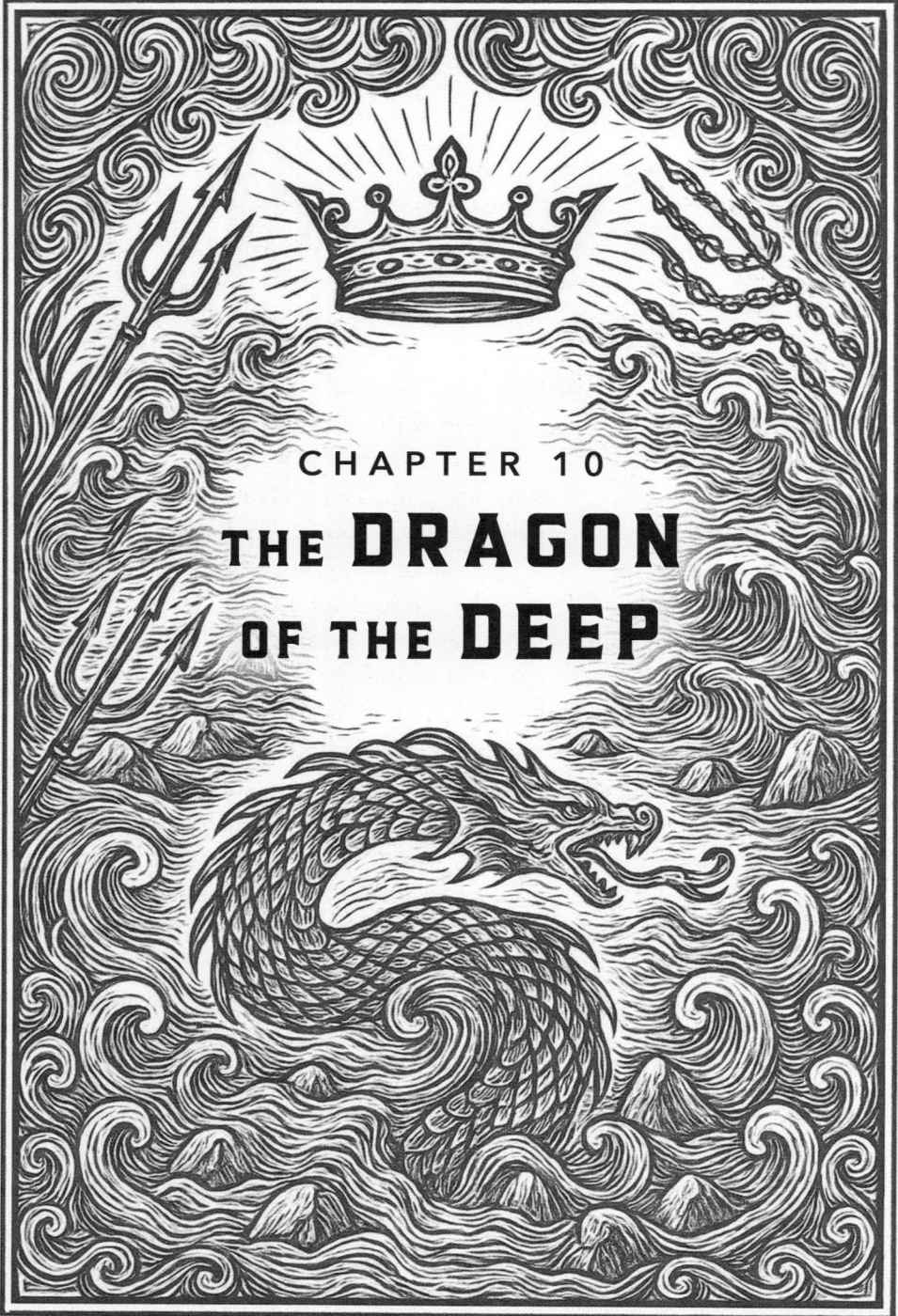

CHAPTER 10

THE **DRAGON** OF THE **DEEP**

IN THE STORY OF THE EXODUS, Pharaoh is much more than a stubborn tyrant—he also serves as an incredibly important prophetic foreshadow. He is described, quite directly by the prophets, poetically as a serpent-king, an earthly vessel of the Devil. Again and again, the Scriptures use imagery and language that frame Pharaoh not merely as an oppressor of Israel but as a monstrous embodiment of Leviathan, the great serpent of the deep. As such, he serves as an archetype—one of the greatest in Scripture, in fact—of the final human adversary: the Antichrist.

THE SERPENT OF THE NILE

From the outset, Egypt's association with the serpent is unmistakable. On the front of Pharaoh's headdress was a prominent cobra called the *uraeus*, a sacred emblem of divine kingship. This was more than a simple decoration. The Egyptians believed the serpent-crested crown empowered the Pharaoh with divine sovereignty and spiritual power. To them, Pharaoh was more than a king—he was a god. Egyptians believed that the Pharaoh was the soul and life force of Egypt.

But in the first act of God's war against Egypt, He commissioned Moses and Aaron to challenge Pharaoh in a very direct manner. When Aaron cast down his staff and it became a serpent (Exod. 7:10), he was not performing some simple parlor trick. He was confronting Pharaoh's divine claim head-on. The staff of God became a living cobra, mimicking the very symbol on Pharaoh's brow. Then, in a dramatic reversal, Aaron's serpent swallowed those of Egypt's magicians! The symbolism would not have been missed by anyone present: YHVH, the God of Israel, consumed Egypt's false gods right before the eyes of their ruler.

The stage was thus set. Egypt and her king were not merely political enemies—they were spiritual enemies. Pharaoh was not just resisting Moses; he was resisting the God of Israel, the One who created the heavens and the earth. Thus, in this story, Pharaoh filled the role of the seed of the serpent, exalted in his pride, determined to crush the people through whom the Deliverer would one day come.

PHAROAH AND MOSES

THE DRAGON IN THE SEA

Beyond the obvious symbolism of the snake worn by Pharaoh, Scripture even directly describes him as a serpent-king. In Ezekiel 29, God speaks directly to Pharaoh:

> "Behold, I am against you,
> Pharaoh, king of Egypt, the great monster [*tannin*: dragon]
> that lies in the midst of his rivers,
> that says, 'My Nile is mine, and I myself have made it.'" (Ezekiel 29:3)

Pharaoh is portrayed here as a king, but also as a dragon thrashing about in the Nile, claiming to own the river, to be the very source of Egypt's life. In a divine warning, God declares that He will put hooks in Pharaoh's jaw and drag him from the river, like a fish dragged out by a fisherman. Then, God says, "I will abandon you in the desert… The beasts of the earth and the birds of the sky will devour you" (v. 5). Pharaoh, as a representative of the great dragon, would be cast down and left to become food for wild scavengers.

In Ezekiel 32, the same imagery returns. There again, Pharaoh is called "a dragon in the seas," a great beast who muddies up the river with his thrashing:

> "You compared yourself to a young lion of the nations, yet you are like
> the monster in the seas; and you burst forth in your rivers and mud-
> died the waters with your feet and fouled their rivers." (Ezekiel 32:2)

But the Lord declares that He will catch this monster in a net, hurl him to the ground, and stain the very mountains with his blood (vv. 2–6):

> "And when I extinguish you, I will cover the heavens and darken their
> stars; I will cover the sun with a cloud and the moon will not give its
> light. All the shining lights in the heavens I will darken over you and
> will set darkness on your land," declares the Lord God. (Ezekiel 32:7–8)

Now, here is where the language becomes apocalyptic. Ezekiel projects Pharaoh's defeat out to the last days. The death of Pharaoh, we are told, will darken the sun and moon and shake the hearts of the nations (vv. 9–10). Every time these cosmic signs appear throughout Scripture, they are always ultimately connected to the Day of the Lord, the end of the age, and the return of Jesus. As Jesus said,

> "But immediately after the tribulation of those days the sun will be darkened, and the moon will not give its light, and the stars will fall from the sky, and the powers of the heavens will be shaken. And then the sign of the Son of Man will appear in the sky, and then all the tribes of the earth will mourn, and they will see the Son of Man coming on the clouds of the sky with power and great glory." (Matthew 24:29–30)

Ezekiel's vision is of cosmic judgment against a king far more consequential than the historical Pharaoh. While it uses him as the type, the ultimate target of the prophecy is the Antichrist.

CRUSHING LEVIATHAN

The Psalms, too, recall Pharaoh's defeat using serpent imagery. In Psalm 74, the exodus is remembered not only as a rescue from bondage but as the slaying of a dragon:

> "You [God] divided the sea by Your strength; You broke the heads of the sea monsters in the waters. You crushed the heads of Leviathan; You gave him as food for the creatures of the wilderness." (Psalm 74:13-14)

In the exodus, Leviathan, the serpent of the sea, was shattered. The Red Sea became the Lord's battlefield upon which He would demonstrate His absolute supremacy. Pharaoh and all his armies, drowned beneath the waters, are cast as sea serpents defeated by the Lord. What is fascinating here is that within the Canaanite myth, it was Baal who was said to have slain the sea serpent. But in a very direct divine taunt, the God of Israel did it in real time and history.

Then in Isaiah 51, the exodus is once again linked with the dragon's defeat. Here, the text refers to Leviathan using the name Rahab:

> "Was it not You who cut Rahab in pieces, Who pierced the dragon?
> Was it not You who dried up the sea, The waters of the great deep?"
> (Isaiah 51:9–10)

Pharaoh, Egypt, and Leviathan all collapse into one symbolic figure: the dragon who opposes God must be slain for God's people to be set free. These passages draw a straight line from the Snake Crusher of Genesis 3 to the banks of the Red Sea—from the Devil himself to the pagan king of Egypt. The enemy may appear in various forms and change names, but Scripture always reveals the consistent spirit behind his many manifestations.

PHARAOH AND THE FINAL BEAST

Although the story of the Exodus is a genuine record of a historical deliverance, it is also a prophetic pattern that points forward to a greater deliverance yet to come at the end of this age.

In Revelation 12, the final dragon will appear one last time. There, Satan is described as "the great dragon," "the serpent of old," who wages war on Israel and her children, just as Pharaoh once did. Like Pharaoh, the dragon stands ready to devour the child born to the woman. And like Moses, the man-child escapes, is hidden for a time, but then returns to crush the enemy.

The imagery not only echoes forward, but also backward. Pharaoh's order to kill the Hebrew boys in Exodus 1 is reflected in Herod's slaughter of the innocents in Matthew 2. In both cases, a dragon seeks to devour the seed. In both cases, God preserves His chosen deliverer. And in both cases, that deliverer returns to lead His people in a mighty

PHAROAH, THE DEFEATED DRAGON OF THE NILE

deliverance. In the case of Jesus, the Greater Moses, the deliverance is not merely from Egypt, but from sin and death itself.

As God once shattered Pharaoh in the sea, so He will one day cast the final beast into the lake of fire (Rev. 19:20). The prototype will find its antitype. The dragon of the Nile becomes the dragon of the Apocalypse. And in both stories, the seed of the woman crushes the serpent.

FROM SEA TO SANCTUARY

This prophetic theme is also reflected in Isaiah 27:

> "In that day the Lord will punish Leviathan the fleeing serpent, With His fierce and great and mighty sword, Even Leviathan the twisted serpent; And He will kill the dragon who lives in the sea." (Isaiah 27:1)

This is the end of the story. The serpent from Eden, the dragon of the Exodus, the beast of the final rebellion—all are slain. And in their place, peace will reign. "They will not hurt or destroy in all My holy mountain" (Isa. 11:9).

THE SERPENT, THE SEA, AND THE SON

Pharaoh, with his serpent crown and hardened heart, was not just Israel's foe—he was the seed of the serpent of that day, energized by the dragon of old. His defeat was a foretaste of the final victory. Just as the serpent was crushed in the sea by the mighty "arm of the Lord," so he will be crushed again—this time not by Moses, but by the Greater Moses. From beginning to end, Scripture tells a single story. Whether in Eden, Egypt, or Revelation, the pattern is always the same: The serpent raises its head to devour the righteous seed-line, but the Lord is a Warrior, *ever and always mighty to save.*

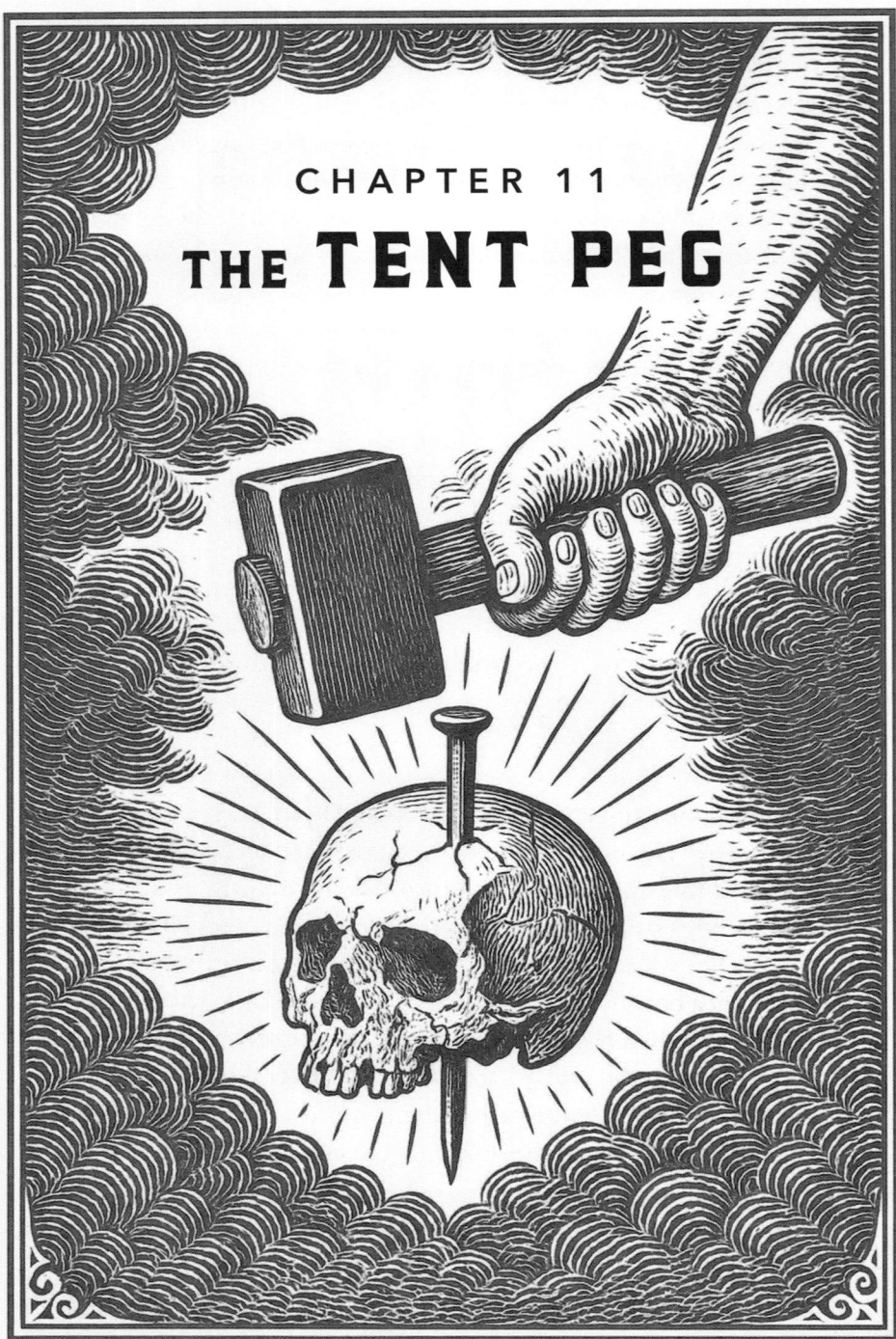

CHAPTER 11
THE **TENT PEG**

FROM THE VERY BEGINNING, as a response to the rebellious audacity of Satan, the promise of God was war. Over and over, that early declaration: "He shall crush your head" echoes throughout the pages of the Bible. The following prophecy is also a promise of both battle and victory for the righteous. Throughout the Scriptures, this war between the seed of the woman and the seed of the serpent plays out again and again in multiple vivid prophetic patterns.

One of the most striking episodes in that war takes place in the days of the Judges—a time of great moral confusion and tribal chaos in Israel. And in that moment, a most unlikely woman rises from obscurity, takes a hammer and a tent peg in her hand, and drives it through the skull of a sleeping enemy commander. Her name was Jael, and her story is more than an act of wartime bravery. It is another powerful shadow of the much greater victory to come.

THE WOMAN IN THE TENT

In Judges 4–5, we read the story of Sisera, the commander of the Canaanite army under King Jabin. The Canaanites were pagans—worshippers of Baal. For twenty years, Sisera had cruelly oppressed the Israelites, boasting nine hundred iron chariots. When the Lord raised up Deborah as a prophetess and Barak as a military leader, the Israelites followed them, raising a rebellion against the Baal worshippers in their midst. Amid this uprising, Sisera was routed in battle.

Fleeing for his life, he came to the tent of Jael, the wife of Heber the Kenite. She welcomed him in. Instead of giving him water, however, she gave him a bowl full of curdled yogurt. Then she covered him with a blanket and lulled him to sleep. With swift resolve, she then took a tent peg in one hand, and a hammer in the other, she crept softly to where he lay, and drove the peg straight through his temple, crushing his skull, and nailing it to the ground (Judges 4:21).

As gruesome as this story may be, the song of Deborah in Judges 5 celebrates it with great enthusiasm:

DEBORAH AND BARAK FIGHT SISERA

"Most blessed of women is Jael, The wife of Heber the Kenite, Most blessed is she of women in the tent. ... She reached out her hand for the tent peg, And her right hand for the workmen's hammer. Then she struck Sisera, she smashed his head; And she shattered and pierced his temple." (Judges 5:24–26)

The language is both graphic and deliberate in its choice of words. She didn't just kill him—she crushed his skull. A prophetic representative of the righteous Seed of the woman strikes again. And though Jael may not have known the full prophetic meaning behind what she had done, the Spirit of God, through her unwavering hands, was proclaiming the Gospel in advance.

ZECHARIAH AND THE TENT PEG FROM JUDAH

Centuries later, the prophet Zechariah would speak of a day when the Lord would again visit His people in battle:

"For the Lord of hosts has visited His flock, the house of Judah, And will make them like His majestic horse in battle. From them will come the cornerstone, *from them the tent peg,* From them the bow of battle, from them every ruler, all of them together." (Zechariah 10:3–4 emphasis added)

Here, the Messiah is described using multiple images—He is the cornerstone, the sure foundation of God's kingdom (cf. Isa. 28:16). He is the bow of battle, the divine warrior who leads the fight. But He is also the tent peg. This is no accident. Zechariah, a prophet thoroughly familiar with the storyline of the Skull Crusher, drew upon the story of Jael to create this beautiful metaphor.

As a prophetic symbol, the Tent Peg is not just a source of stability—it is a weapon. In the hands of the faithful, it became an instrument of judgment. Jael's tent peg was the definitive strike that ended Sisera's reign of terror. The Messiah, too, will wield judgment, and the enemy He defeats will not be just a local warlord—he will be the final Antichrist, the serpent-king of the last days.

THE ANTICHRIST: A NEW SISERA

Like Pharaoh before him, Sisera is not just a man—he is a shadow. He is a forerunner of the final enemy, the last of the serpent's seed. Like Pharaoh, Sisera is also a tyrant and enemy of God who exalts himself against the Lord and His people.

As the Apostle Paul warns, the coming "man of lawlessness" will exalt himself above every so-called god and take his seat in the Jewish temple, "displaying himself as being God" (2 Thess. 2:4). Like Sisera, he will unleash a reign of terror. Like Sisera, he will seem invincible. And like Sisera, he too will fall.

The story of Jael points forward and gives us hope concerning that final day. Revelation 19 tells us that the Messiah—the true and better Tent Peg—will return riding a white horse, with a sword proceeding from His mouth, with eyes like an inferno.

BETWEEN HER FEET HE BOWED

The closing lines of Deborah's song are hauntingly poetic:

> "Between her feet he bowed, he fell, he lay; Between her feet he bowed, he fell; Where he bowed, there he fell dead." (Judges 5:27)

The repetition drives home the humiliation of the serpent's seed. Between the feet of a woman—the figure God said would bring forth the deliverer—he falls in defeat. In this way, Jael becomes a prophetic witness, a living parable of the gospel. She is not the Seed of the woman, but her hand would bear witness to the coming victory of the ultimate Skull Crusher.

THE TENT PEG AND THE NAIL

It is no accident that the Messiah's greatest victory—His own death— was also accomplished with nails. At the cross, the Seed of the woman was bruised. His hands and feet were pierced. He was crushed for our iniquities. But through that very piercing, the serpent's head was struck. Colossians 2 tells us that at the cross, Jesus "disarmed the rulers and authorities" and "made a public display of them, having triumphed over them" (Col. 2:15). The enemy thought that he was crushing the Seed. In reality, it was through Roman hammers and spikes that Satan's defeat was forever sealed.

BLESSED AMONG WOMEN

Deborah declared, "Most blessed among women is Jael." But centuries later, an angel would echo similar words to a young Jewish girl: "Blessed are you among women, and blessed is the fruit of your womb!" (Luke 1:42). Jael's hand struck a blow against the serpent. Mary's womb brought forth the One who would crush him forever. Jesus is the true Tent Peg. He is the One Zechariah foresaw, the One Jael foreshadowed, and the One Deborah sang about. He is the Seed whose crushing has guaranteed Satan's future and final judgment. When Jesus comes again, He will not merely strike another earthly tyrant—he will bind the great Dragon, eventually casting him into hell forever. Between Jesus' feet, the serpent will both bow and fall.

THE TENT PEG

CHAPTER 12

THE **MESSIAH**

THE PERIOD OF THE JUDGES were dark days for Israel. They had no king. Every man did what was right in his own eyes. But into this bleak landscape, God once again spoke hope—this time through the cry of a barren woman. Her name was Hannah. She was visiting the Tabernacle at Shiloh, where the ark of the covenant was kept during this period. Through tears and much pain, Hannah prayed to the Lord, and He heard her cry. The Lord opened her womb, and she gave birth to a son—Samuel, the prophet who would anoint kings. But it was what Hannah sang after the birth that would echo through the ages. Her song, recorded in 1 Samuel 2, is far more than a song of praise to God—it is also a prophecy. The song of Hannah is laced with the promises of justice and judgment, of lifting the lowly and crushing the proud. It is a song that looks forward to a king—a *Messiah*—and a day when God Himself will rise to judge the earth.

THE SONG OF THE BARREN WOMAN

Hannah begins her song, not lamenting her pain, but by extolling God's nature:

> "There is no one holy like the Lord, Indeed, there is no one besides You, Nor is there any rock like our God" (1 Samuel 2:2).

From the start, she draws our attention upward. Then, her vindication becomes a window into a much grander vision. Her words pulse with the pattern of divine reversal and justice:

> "Those who were full hire themselves out for bread,
> But those who were hungry cease to hunger.
> Even the barren gives birth to seven,
> But she who has many children languishes" (v. 5).

This is the God who flips the world upside down—who brings justice to the poor and suffering.

HANNAH'S SONG

RESURRECTION, JUDGMENT, AND THE COMING ONE

At the center of Hannah's prayer is a startling declaration:

> "The Lord kills and makes alive;
> He brings down to Sheol and raises up" (v. 6).

This is speaking of resurrection. Long before Ezekiel would proclaim the raising of dry bones or the defeat of death, Hannah saw it. The same God who humbles also exalts. The same God who judges also saves. One can even feel the reverberations of the promise of Genesis 3:15—that one would be wounded, will rise up to crush the serpent.

But Hannah's vision expands beyond personal deliverance or even national restoration. Her closing words erupt with prophetic thunder:

> "The adversaries of the Lord will be broken to pieces; Against them
> He will thunder in the heavens... The Lord will judge the ends of the
> earth; And He will give strength to His king, And will exalt the horn
> of His anointed [Messiah]" (vv. 10).

This is not just a simple call for moral justice—it is a cosmic vision. The same God who brought justice for the barren woman will execute justice for the whole earth. Here, Hannah draws on the very imagery of Enoch's prophecy, where the Lord comes with ten thousands of His holy ones to execute judgment upon all (Jude 14–15). She channels the words of Moses in his final blessing over Israel, in which the Lord comes from Sinai with lightning flashing from His hands. (Deut 33:2). Here He is again, thundering from heaven. Moses described the God of Israel descending with fire, in a cloud, with an army of holy ones to judge and to save. Hannah picks up the same theme. Her God will come with thunder, riding across the heavens to judge the ends of the earth. Hannah saw the Skull Crusher as not only the Seed but the Sovereign God of heaven.

THE LORD THUNDERS FROM HEAVEN

THE FIRST MENTION OF MESSIAH

Hannah's final words are explosive:

> "He will give strength to His king, And exalt the horn of His anointed" (v. 10).

This is the first time in Scripture that the word *Messiah* (*moshiach*) is used in prophetic anticipation. Israel had no king yet. Like those who came before her, Hannah prophesied the kingdom before it existed. Her words anticipated David, but they also saw beyond him. She saw the rise of a King who would not merely rule Israel but judge the earth.

Hannah's prophetic song fuses the two messianic streams: the Skull Crusher of Genesis 3:15 and the Cloud-Rider of Deuteronomy 33. One is born of the woman to crush the serpent. The other descends from heaven to crush the nations. In Hannah's vision, they converge.

THE PATTERN CONTINUES

In the previous prophecy, we saw Jael—another woman—lift her hand to strike the head of the enemy. Through her courage, the Lord delivered Israel. Hannah continues this theme, but her weapon is a song. Her voice, like Jael's hammer, delivers a prophetic blow to the powers of darkness. Her prophecy, like all those that came before her, offers hope during a season of hopelessness. Her son Samuel will go on to anoint the first kings of Israel. But the true King, the Skull Crusher, the King who thunders in the heavens, is still to come. Hannah has given us the melody. Soon, we will hear the first movements of the royal march. As the battle builds, once again, God has spoken through the lowly to announce the downfall of the proud.

CHAPTER 13

THE SERPENT of GATH

AS WE ARE BEGINNING TO SEE, the ancient promise given in Eden—that the seed of the woman would crush the head of the serpent (Genesis 3:15)—is not a footnote in redemptive history. It is the very backbone of the entire biblical storyline. Thus it resurfaces yet again, with chilling clarity, this time in the valley of Elah.

Most readers have heard the story of David and Goliath. They know it as a lesson in courage, faith, or perhaps as an inspiring story of an underdog winning an unlikely victory. The deeper truth, however, one that has been largely missed, is that this historical skirmish is yet another prophetic foreshadowing. It is an echo or a signpost along the way to the ultimate fulfillment. The battle between David and Goliath is a reenactment of sorts—a shadow of the ultimate showdown between the Messiah and the Antichrist. Goliath, however, is no ordinary warrior. He is portrayed as a monstrous, serpentine figure—a dragon in bronze scales. Similarly, David is more than a shepherd boy. He is the anointed of the Lord. The serpent rises, the seed is revealed, and once more, the head is crushed.

THE ARMOR OF A BEAST

The author of 1 Samuel devotes an unusual amount of space to describing Goliath's armor. Verse after verse paints a somewhat other-worldly picture. First, Goliath is over nine feet tall. He is also cloaked in "scaly armor" of bronze, a term elsewhere used in the Old Testament exclusively for fish and sea monsters (cf. Ezekiel 29:3–4). In fact, Goliath and Pharaoh are the only two characters in all of Scripture who are described with "scales." In Ezekiel, Pharaoh was likened to a sea dragon—Leviathan. In Samuel, the same serpentine imagery reemerges in Goliath. He is a giant sea dragon walking on dry land.

The armor is more than military protection—it is also symbolic. Four times we're told that Goliath's gear is made of bronze, a Hebrew word that sounds very close to the Hebrew word for serpent. This is not a coincidence. The author deliberately echoes the bronze serpent Moses lifted up in the wilderness (Numbers 21:9). Goliath is presented as the

DAVID AND GOLIATH

living embodiment of the serpent, taunting and hissing in rebellious mockery against the God of Israel.

A CHAMPION OF REBELLION

Goliath is introduced not simply as a warrior, but as the *ish ha-benayim*—literally, "the man of the in-between" (1 Samuel 17:4). This is a strange phrase, found nowhere else in Scripture. While it may refer to his role as a champion between two armies, the phrase also subtly evokes Genesis 3:15, where God declares He will put *enmity* "between" the seed of the woman and the seed of the serpent.

Goliath is more than a soldier; he is the embodiment of that enmity. He is the serpent's champion—towering, boastful, clothed in scales, defying the armies of God. But he is much more than a garden variety rebel. Goliath is also a giant. A descendant of the Rephaim, he belongs to the ancient race of giants—those who descended from the Nephilim, the offspring of the rebellious "sons of God" and the daughters of men in Genesis 6. These beings were not just physical aberrations; they were the fruit of a cosmic insurrection.

Thus, Goliath does not merely represent the serpent of Eden, but also the heavenly rebellion. Goliath is a composite symbol of the two great rebellions that scarred creation: Satan's deceit in the garden and the defilement of humanity in the days of Noah. He is the convergence of the serpent and the sons of God who came down—the perfect type of the final Beast, who will unite the deception of Eden with the defiance of the Watchers.

In Goliath, the serpent seed and the rebel sons of heaven come together in flesh and bronze. This is what David faces—not merely a man, but a representative of all that is evil and defiant.

THE STRIKE HEARD ROUND THE WORLD

David, the shepherd boy, steps into the valley. He carries no sword, no armor, no spear—only a sling and five smooth stones. And yet he utters what is perhaps the most stirring war cry in all of the Old Testament:

"You come to me with a sword, a spear, and a javelin, but I come to you in the name of the Lord of Hosts, the God of the armies of Israel, whom you have taunted… that all this assembly may know that the Lord does not deliver by sword or by spear; for the battle is the Lord's, and He will give you into our hands" (1 Samuel 17:45,47).

And then it happens. The stone flies. It sinks into Goliath's forehead. The giant falls face down, mouth in the dust (Genesis 3:14). David runs forward and, with Goliath's own sword, removes his head. This is not subtle imagery. A scaled monster is struck in the head by a humble anointed one. The serpent thumps his chest and mocks, but with nearly no effort, the seed crushes. As another sign along the way to the final victory, we are reminded that the promise of the ultimate triumph still stands.

DAVID THE SEED-BEARER

In keeping with the symbolism, David is not the Messiah, but he is a picture of Him. Like Jesus, David is anointed by God, rejected by men, and raised up to save his people. He wins a decisive battle on behalf of the nation while they stand helpless and afraid. His victory then becomes their victory.

The battle with Goliath is not primarily about technique, tactics, or nerve. It is about calling and covenant. David stepped forward with confidence because he knew the promise: the serpent would be crushed. And he knows who God is: "The battle belongs to the Lord."

Just as Jesus would later step into the battlefield of Golgotha unarmed, one Jewish man against the world, so also did David step into the valley armed only with faith and a few smooth stones. And just as the stone struck the beast's head, so too, at the cross, was the fate of the enemy sealed.

DAVID SLAYS GOLIATH

A FORESHADOWING OF FINAL VICTORY

The story of David and Goliath is not just an ancient story to be read in Sunday School. It is another glimpse of God's eschatological blueprint. Goliath is a shadow of the final beast, the Antichrist—a proud, blasphemous, serpent-like tyrant who will rise to challenge the armies of the living God. David is the foreshadow of the returning Son of David—the true Messiah, who will strike the beast with the breath of His mouth and destroy him by the brightness of His coming (2 Thessalonians 2:8).

This is the heartbeat of hope that beats through the entire Bible— the hope that one day, the true and greater David will rise, not merely to slay a giant, but to crush the final dragon, to silence all blasphemies, and establish a kingdom that will have no end.

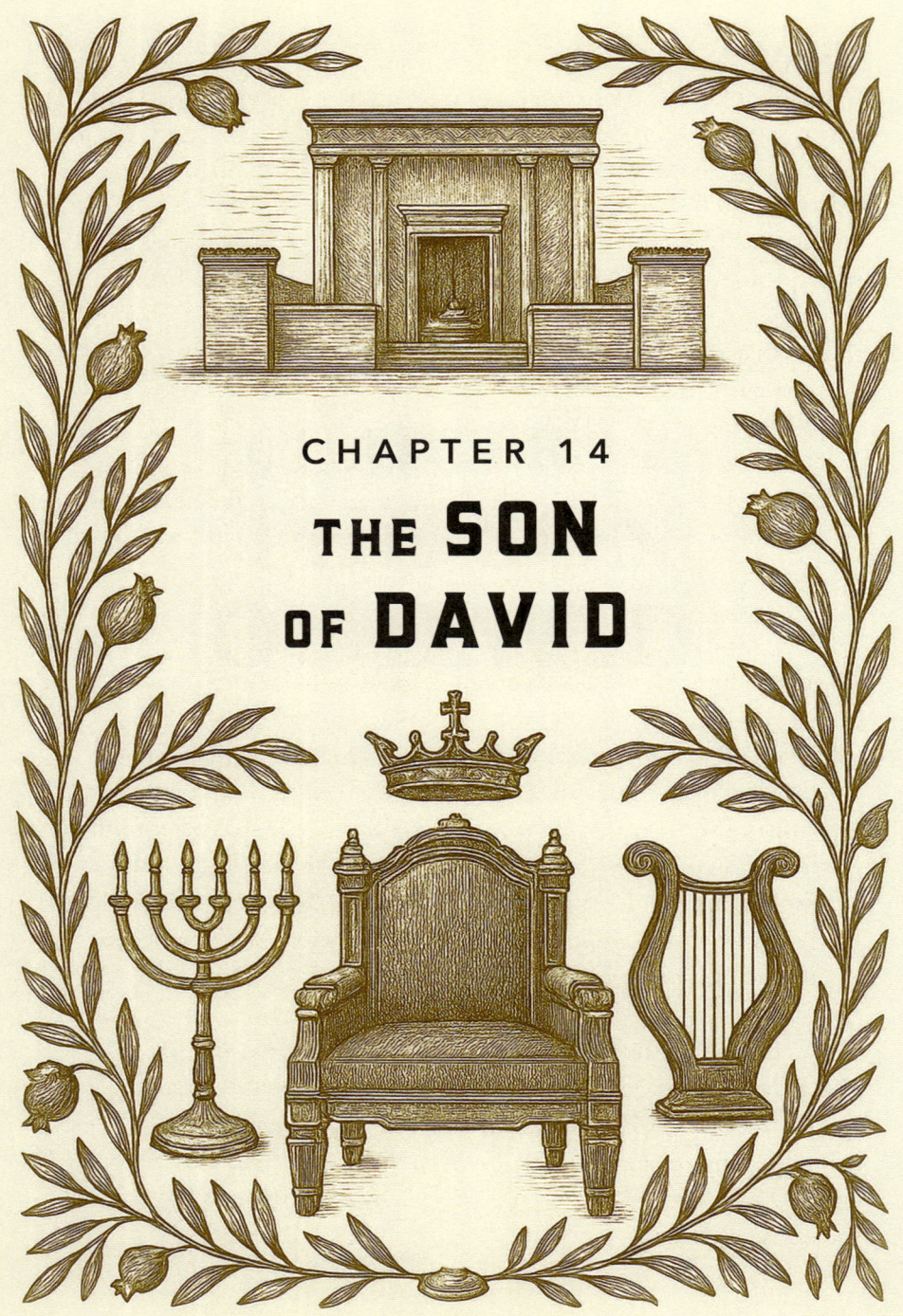

CHAPTER 14

THE **SON** OF **DAVID**

THE NEXT MAJOR PROPHECY concerning the coming King was given hundreds of years after Abraham, during the reign of King David. By this time, Israel had entered the land, and David was ruling from Jerusalem. The Scriptures tell us, "The Lord had given him rest on every side from all his enemies" (2 Sam 7:1). In this moment of peace and national stability, the Lord made a covenant with David—one of the most profound and far-reaching covenants in the entire Bible.

It begins with a reaffirmation of the land promises first made to Abraham and reiterated to Moses in the Abrahamic and Mosaic Covenants:

> "I will also appoint a place for My people Israel and will plant them, that they may live in their own place and not be disturbed again, nor will the wicked afflict them any more as formerly... and I will give you rest from all your enemies" (2 Samuel 7:10–11).

How would God accomplish this lasting peace and security for Israel? Through a future king, a descendant, a "seed"—from David's own body:

> "The LORD also declares to you that the LORD will make a house for you. When your days are complete and you lie down with your fathers, I will raise up your descendant after you, who will come forth from you, and I will establish his kingdom. He shall build a house for My name, and I will establish the throne of his kingdom forever... Your house and your kingdom shall endure before Me forever; your throne shall be established forever" (2 Samuel 7:12–16).

Here, the divine promise narrows yet again. We saw the promise first given to Eve, then through the family of Shem. Abraham, Isaac, and Jacob were each told that their "seed" would inherit the land and bring blessing to the nations. It was then revealed that the seed would come specifically from the tribe of Judah. Now the spotlight falls on the house of David.

NATHAN CONVEYS THE DAVIDIC COVENANT

The coming King would inherit David's throne, rule over a kingdom, and reign forever. But for a kingdom to endure forever, its King must live forever. The hope of Israel became a never-ending kingdom ruled by an immortal King, one who would build a house for God and dwell among His people. Though fully human, the seed of David is once again revealed to be far more than a man. He is also divine.

PSALM 2: THE ANOINTED SON

Psalm 2 is one of the most foundational messianic prophecies in the entire Bible. Authored by David under the inspiration of the Holy Spirit (Acts 4:25), it offers a vision of global rebellion and divine rule. Charles Spurgeon aptly called it *"The Psalm of Messiah the Prince."*

It begins with the nations raging in futility:

"Why are the nations in an uproar And the peoples devising a vain thing? The kings of the earth take their stand And the rulers take counsel together Against the LORD and against His Anointed."

Here we encounter the word "Anointed," which means "Messiah." First introduced in Hannah's song, here it is again applied to the Promised One. The nations rage against His rule, crying out:

"Let us tear their fetters apart And cast away their cords from us!"

But God is unmoved. From His heavenly throne, He responds with divine derision:

"He who sits in the heavens laughs, The Lord scoffs at them. Then He will speak to them in His anger And terrify them in His fury, saying, 'But as for Me, I have installed My King Upon Zion, My holy mountain.'"

The focus then shifts to the Anointed One Himself, who declares:

"I will surely tell of the decree of the LORD: He said to Me, 'You are My Son, Today I have begotten You. Ask of Me, and I will surely give the nations as Your inheritance, And the very ends of the earth as Your possession. You shall break them with a rod of iron, You shall shatter them like earthenware.'"

This is no ordinary king. He is God's own Son, begotten by divine decree. The New Testament cites this psalm (Heb 1:5) to emphasize the divine identity of Jesus the Messiah. He is not merely a ruler of Israel—He will inherit all nations. His reign will be absolute.

The psalm ends with a warning to the rulers of the earth:

"Now therefore, O kings, show discernment; Take warning, O judges of the earth. Worship the LORD with reverence And rejoice with trembling. Do homage to the Son, that He not become angry, And you perish in the way… How blessed are all who take refuge in Him!"

PSALM 72: THE KINGDOM OF PEACE AND GLORY

Psalm 72, attributed to David or Solomon, is a royal prayer—a prophetic cry for the reign of the Messiah:

"Give the king Your judgments, O God, And Your righteousness to the king's son. May he judge Your people with righteousness And Your afflicted with justice" (vv. 1–2).

This King will bring justice for the poor and oppressed. He will not only vindicate the afflicted—He will crush the oppressor:

"May he vindicate the afflicted of the people, Save the children of the needy And crush the oppressor" (v. 4).

HE WILL CRUSH KINGS ON THE DAY OF HIS WRATH

HE WILL DRINK FROM THE BROOK BY THE WAY

His dominion is global and everlasting:

"May he also rule from sea to sea And from the River to the ends of the earth. Let all kings bow down before him, All nations serve him... May his name endure forever... And may the whole earth be filled with His glory" (vv. 8–11, 17–19).

The legendary preacher Charles Spurgeon summed up the essence of this royal psalm well:

"Widespread shall be the rule of Messiah... From Pacific to Atlantic, and from Atlantic to Pacific, He shall be Lord, and the oceans which surround each pole shall be beneath His sway. All other power shall be subordinate to His."

PSALM 102: THE LORD APPEARS IN GLORY

Psalm 102 begins as a cry for mercy but crescendos into a stunning messianic vision:

"You will arise and have compassion on Zion; For it is time to be gracious to her... So the nations will fear the name of the Lord And all the kings of the earth Your glory. For the LORD has built up Zion; He has appeared in His glory" (Psalm 102:13–16).

Unlike many messianic passages that describe God's agent, this one presents God Himself appearing in His glory. The Messiah is not merely the representative of God—He is God in the flesh. The ancient Israelites may not have grasped the full implications, but the truth was there: the Promised One would be YHVH Himself coming to redeem His people.

I HAVE INSTALLED MY KING ON MOUNT ZION

PSALM 110: THE PRIEST-KING

Psalm 110 stands alongside Psalm 2 as one of the most explicit messianic declarations in all of Scripture. Jesus Himself cited this psalm to reveal the divine identity of the Messiah (Matt 22:41–45):

> "The LORD says to my Lord: 'Sit at My right hand Until I make Your enemies a footstool for Your feet.' The LORD will stretch forth Your strong scepter from Zion, saying, 'Rule in the midst of Your enemies'" (vv. 1–2).

Christians understand this heavenly discourse to have taken place between God the Father and God the Son. There is a clear distinction in the divine persons, since one speaks to another; yet they are also One. The divinity of the Messiah is demonstrated by the fact that David called his son "my Lord" (literally *Adonai*).

David understood that his promised "son" was much more than a mere man.

The Anointed One is told to sit at YHVH's right hand until the appointed time arrives for Him to establish His throne on Mount Zion and rule over His enemies.

The language of making His enemies a footstool under His feet reflects the idea of crushing them under His feet. All of the most common themes of the previous messianic prophecies are here. The King of Israel will crush the enemies of God.

In accordance with the warning of Psalm 2, every knee will bow before the Messiah, and to the very ends of the earth, they will all confess that He is Lord.

Next, we're told that His people will freely give themselves to His cause:

> Your people will volunteer freely in the day of Your power;
> In holy array, from the womb of the dawn,
> Your youth are to You as the dew. (v. 3)

The citizens of the coming kingdom will enthusiastically join with Him and His cause. Reminiscent of the Lord's promise to Abraham to multiply his descendants until they become as numerous as the stars of the sky, the volunteers here are as vast in number as the dew droplets of the morning, having come forth from the very "womb of the dawn."

Then comes a surprising revelation. The Messiah is not only a king who will rule forever, but also a priest forever:

> "The LORD has sworn and will not change His mind, 'You are a priest forever According to the order of Melchizedek'" (v. 4).

The Messiah will be a priestly mediator between God and man according to the order of Melchizedek, the priest-king who lived in Abraham's day (Gen. 14:18–20). His name means "king of righteousness," and as the king of Salem (which later became known as Jerusalem), he was also the "king of peace." So also will Messiah be a priest and the King of Righteousness and Peace.

The psalm ends with a terrifying picture of final judgment:

> "He will shatter kings in the day of His wrath. He will judge among the nations, He will fill them with corpses, He will shatter the chief men over a broad country" (vv. 5–6).

This is the language of conquest. The Skull Crusher will crush not only the serpent, but every power that opposes God.

And yet, He is undeterred:

> "He will drink from the brook by the wayside; Therefore He will lift up His head" (v. 7).

Like a battle-hardened warrior pausing to drink before marching on, He is focused, unwavering, and victorious.

CONCLUSION

Following the Exodus, Israel's messianic hope centered more clearly on the coming King, the Son of David. Through God's covenant with David and the psalms that followed, a breathtaking portrait emerged: a divine, eternal King who would rule with justice, crush every oppressor, and reign in righteousness and peace.

He is the Anointed One, God's own Son, the inheritor of the nations. He is the Priest-King who mediates between heaven and earth, and the Warrior-King who judges the wicked. The Seed of David is the Skull Crusher of Eden—a Jewish man and the Lord of glory who will reign from Zion.

This is the hope of Israel. This is the hope of the nations. The One to whom every knee will bow.

CHAPTER 15

THE **BRANCH**

AFTER THE REIGNS of King David and his son Solomon, the kingdom's glory quickly faded, and the nation was divided into two separate kingdoms. Israel became its own kingdom in the Galilee, separate from Judah in the south. Eventually, both kingdoms were attacked, defeated, and their people deported—Israel by Assyria, and Judah by Babylon. The unbroken line of Davidic kings met its end when Nebuchadnezzar captured Jerusalem and, in a brutal act of finality, slaughtered the sons of Zedekiah, the last king of Judah, before his very eyes. Then, in a haunting display of defeat, he burned out Zedekiah's eyes, bound him with bronze fetters, and dragged him off to Babylon in utter humiliation (2 Kings 25:7). To those looking on, it may have seemed that the covenant promise of God had failed. The glorious tree of David's Kingdom had become a stump. The throne of David was empty. The glory had departed.

Yet throughout this period, the prophets continued to carry the flame of hope. They continued to speak of the King who was to come, but they also began describing the nature of His kingdom with incredible detail. What would the messianic reign look like? What would the world become during those days? The prophets consistently portrayed it as a golden age—an era resembling both a restored Garden of Eden and the glory days of David's kingdom combined. This future dominion would not be confined to the borders of the promised land; it would extend to the very ends of the earth. The restoration they foretold was comprehensive: national, political, spiritual, and global.

During this same time, the prophets increasingly used the word "Zion" to describe the center of this restored creation. But they spoke of it in distant, eschatological terms, using phrases like "in the latter days," "the last days," or simply "in that day." They also began to speak more clearly about the apocalyptic judgment that would precede the messianic age. This climactic event they called "The Day of the Lord." By the first century, during the ministries of Jesus and the apostles, each of these themes—Zion, the Day of the Lord, the Branch, the Messiah—had become firmly rooted in Jewish expectation. To rightly understand the mindset of Jesus and His contemporaries, we must become familiar with these prophetic passages and the ideas they communicate.

ISAIAH 2-4

The most prolific prophet of restoration was Isaiah. His writings include some of the most stirring and sublime descriptions of the coming kingdom in all of Scripture. His first major prophecy about the messianic kingdom, spanning Isaiah chapters 2–4, offers a vivid picture of what the earth will be like during the Messiah's reign. The context is set in the opening verse: "In the last days."

> The mountain of the house of the Lord Will be established as the chief of the mountains, And will be raised above the hills; And all the nations will stream to it. (Isaiah 2:2)

Here, Israel is envisioned as the highest mountain in the world, with all other nations portrayed as lesser hills. People from every nation will flow like rivers to Zion, eager to learn from God:

> And many peoples will come and say, "Come, let us go up to the mountain of the Lord, To the house of the God of Jacob; That He may teach us concerning His ways And that we may walk in His paths." For the law will go forth from Zion And the word of the Lord from Jerusalem.

God Himself will be present, governing, teaching, and giving counsel to the whole earth:

> And He will judge between the nations, And will render decisions for many peoples; And they will hammer their swords into plowshares And their spears into pruning hooks. Nation will not lift up sword against nation, And never again will they learn war. (v. 4)

As a result of His leadership, wars will cease, and the earth will be filled with peace. In this agrarian utopia, the people of the earth will repurpose their weapons into tools of cultivation.

The phrase "in that day" appears six times throughout these chapters (2:11, 17, 20; 3:18; 4:1–2), linking them together. Isaiah then makes a direct reference to the Messiah:

> In that day the Branch of the Lord will be beautiful and glorious, and the fruit of the earth will be the pride and adornment of the survivors of Israel. (Isaiah 4:2)

THE BRANCH

Here, Isaiah introduces a new title for the Messiah: "The Branch" (*tsemach* in Hebrew). Later prophets would adopt and expand this imagery (see Jer. 23:5; 33:15; Zech. 3:8; 6:12). In some instances, He is called "the Branch of David," indicating His human descent from David's royal line. But here, He is "the Branch of the Lord," pointing to His divine origin. The Messiah springs from a dual lineage—He is both Son of David and Son of God.

In Zechariah, one of the last prophetic voices of the Old Testament, this title is used again with remarkable clarity. Astonishingly, the prophetic model for this future King is a man named Joshua—Yeshua in Hebrew, the same name as Jesus:

> Take silver and gold, make an ornate crown and set it on the head of Joshua the son of Jehozadak, the high priest. Then say to him, "Thus says the Lord of hosts, 'Behold, a man whose name is Branch, for He will branch out from where He is; and He will build the temple of the Lord. Yes, it is He who will build the temple of the Lord, and He who will bear the honor and sit and rule on His throne. Thus, He will be a priest on His throne, and the counsel of peace will be between the two offices." (Zechariah 6:11–13)

THE BRANCH OF DAVID

This coming King is described as both priest and ruler, and He will build the temple of God in Jerusalem.

ISAIAH 9:6-7

Isaiah 9 contains one of the most beloved and well-known messianic prophecies in the entire Bible. Addressed to the northern kingdom of Israel—the land of Zebulun and Naphtali, near the Sea of Galilee—it speaks to a people devastated by Assyrian conquest and exile. Though the region was enveloped in gloom, a radiant hope was promised:

> But there will be no more gloom for her who was in anguish; in earlier times He treated the land of Zebulun and Naphtali with contempt, but later on He shall make it glorious, by the way of the sea, on the other side of the Jordan, Galilee of the Gentiles. The people who walk in darkness will see a great light; Those who live in a dark land, the light will shine on them. (vv. 1–2)

Despite the devastation and depopulation, joy will be restored. And what is this light? What will bring such gladness?

> For a child will be born to us, a son will be given to us; And the government will rest on His shoulders; And His name will be called Wonderful Counselor, Mighty God, Eternal Father, Prince of Peace. (v. 6)

This child, foretold earlier as the virgin-born "Immanuel" (Isa. 7:14), is described with divine titles: *El Gibbor*—"Mighty God," Wonderful Counselor, and Prince of Peace. Though born as a man, He is God in the flesh. "Eternal Father" refers not to the first person of the Trinity, but to the Messiah's fatherly care over His people. These names together describe one who is both fully divine and truly human—the perfect image of God.

There will be no end to the increase of His government or of peace, On the throne of David and over His kingdom, To establish it and to uphold it with justice and righteousness From then on and forevermore. (v. 7a)

As foretold in God's covenant with David (2 Sam. 7:12–13), the Messiah will sit on David's throne forever. Isaiah assures us that this vision will come to pass: "The zeal of the Lord of hosts will accomplish this." (v. 7b)

RESTORATION

In Isaiah chapter 11, the prophet returns to the image of a tree to describe David's dynasty—a tree cut down, leaving only a stump. But hope is not lost:

Then a shoot will spring from the stem of Jesse, And a branch from his roots will bear fruit. (v. 1)

Though the royal line appeared dead, a new shoot—a Branch, would arise. Upon Him, the Spirit of the Lord would rest in full measure:

The Spirit of the Lord will rest on Him, The spirit of wisdom and understanding, The spirit of counsel and strength, The spirit of knowledge and the fear of the Lord. (v. 2)

Seven qualities are listed, signifying divine fullness and perfection.

But with righteousness He will judge the poor, And decide with fairness for the afflicted of the earth; And He will strike the earth with the rod of His mouth, And with the breath of His lips He will slay the wicked. (v. 4)

This King defends the oppressed and strikes the wicked with His very word. Paul later cites this passage to describe Jesus slaying the Antichrist at His return (2 Thess. 2:8).

Then follows one of the most beloved images of the messianic age:

> The wolf will dwell with the lamb … The lion will eat straw like the ox … The nursing child will play by the hole of the cobra … (vv. 6–8)

Nature itself will be transformed. The earth will be renewed, Eden restored.

> For the earth will be full of the knowledge of the Lord As the waters cover the sea. Then in that day The nations will resort to the root of Jesse … (vv. 9–10)

Strikingly, the Messiah is called not only Jesse's shoot but also his root. He comes after David, yet He also existed before him. As Jesus would later declare, "Before Abraham was born, I am" (John 8:58).

MICAH 5

The prophet Micah also contributed key details. He wrote:

> But as for you, Bethlehem Ephrathah, Too little to be among the clans of Judah, From you One will go forth for Me to be ruler in Israel. His goings forth are from long ago, From the days of eternity. (v. 2)

About five miles southwest of Jerusalem, Bethlehem was the birthplace of King David (1 Sam 16:1, 18; 17:12). Here, we're told that despite its small-town stature and relative insignificance, it would also produce the long-awaited Messiah. It is from this verse, of course, that the writer of the Christmas carol "O Little Town of Bethlehem" found his inspiration. The King would become the ruler of all of Israel, unifying the northern and southern kingdoms. As in other previous

ZECHARIAH CROWNS OF JOSHUA THE HIGH PRIEST

messianic passages, the Messiah's preexistence (from "long ago" and "days of eternity") is declared. Although His origins extend back into eternity, His coming to rule remained in the future.

The remainder of the prophecy speaks of the Lord giving Israel up to suffer at the hands of her enemies, "until the time when she who is in labor has borne a child" (v. 3). When the King comes, "He will arise and shepherd His flock in the strength of the Lord, in the majesty of the name of the Lord His God" (v. 4). He is described as delivering Israel militarily from the efforts of foreign invaders and occupying forces. (v. 5). In those days, the "remnant" of Israel will be victorious over her enemies, "Like a lion among the beasts of the forest, like a young lion among flocks of sheep" (v. 8). All of her enemies "will be cut off" (v. 9). The King will, "execute vengeance in anger and wrath on the nations which have not obeyed" (v. 15).

CONCLUSION

After the exile and apparent collapse of David's royal line, the prophets never gave up on Israel's hope. They revealed that the Messiah would be born in Bethlehem, would be a blessing to the Galilee, would sit on David's throne, and reign over a restored, Eden-like world. He would be both human and divine, called "Mighty God" and acting as God's representative on earth. He would be the Branch, the Shoot, and the Root of Jesse—all of the above. Even though His kingdom was still far off, in the mind of the prophets, it was certain. The prophets spoke of the coming Kingdom with tremendous hope, eagerly describing its arrival "in the latter days." These visions form the backbone of Jewish expectation during Jesus's day—and they must continue to remain the central hope of His followers today.

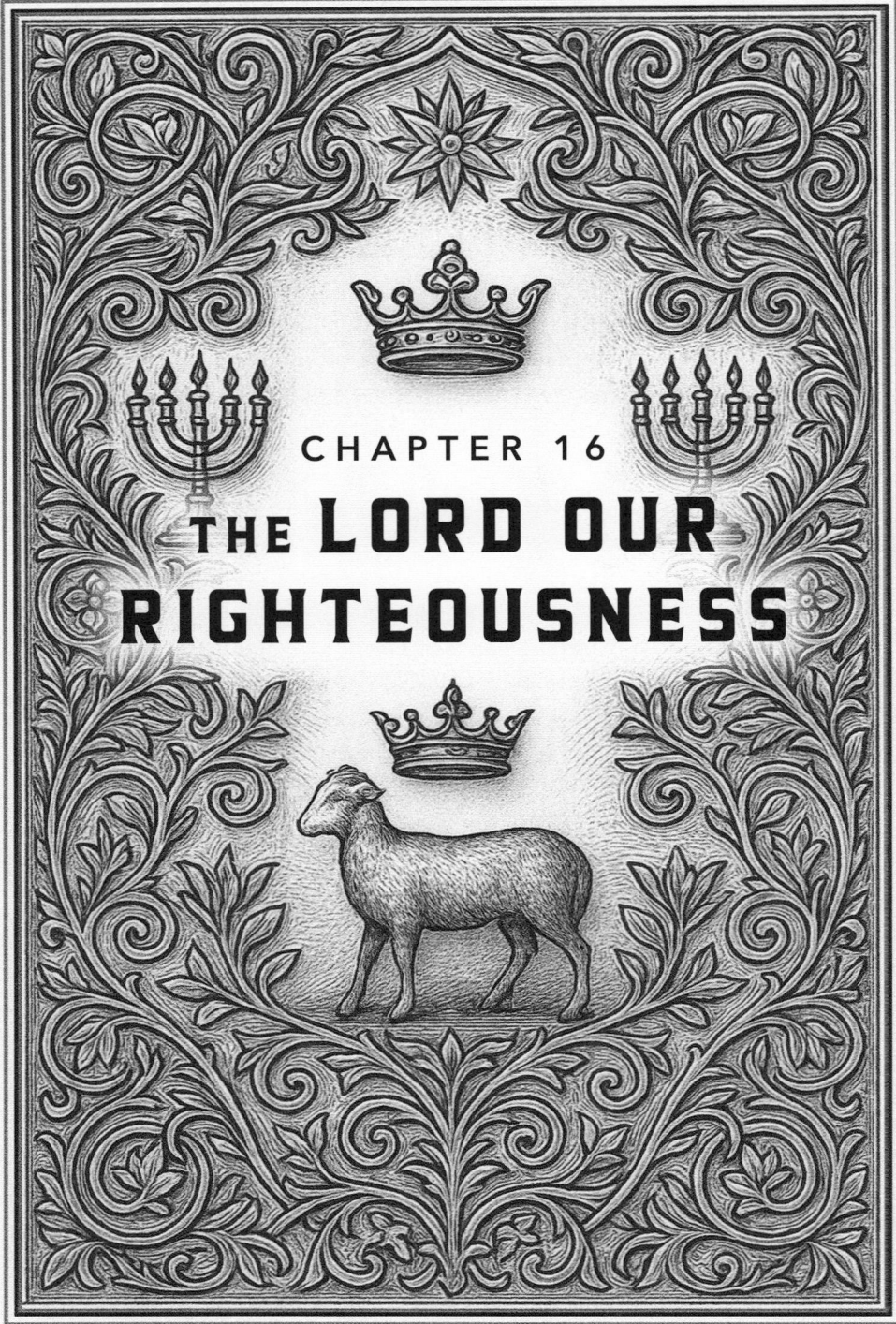

CHAPTER 16

THE LORD OUR RIGHTEOUSNESS

BEYOND ISAIAH'S PROPHECIES about the branch who will restore the throne of David, Jeremiah also prophesied about the Righteous Branch. It was in the midst of one of Judah's darkest periods that the Lord gave Jeremiah a breathtaking glimpse of hope. His prophecy not only reaffirms the promise of a coming King from David's line—it also provides one of the most clear and straightforward affirmations of the Messiah's divine nature in the entire Old Testament:

> "Behold, the days are coming," declares the Lord, "when I will raise up for David a righteous Branch; And He will reign as king and act wisely And do justice and righteousness in the land. In His days Judah will be saved, And Israel will dwell securely; And this is His name by which He will be called: 'The Lord Our Righteousness" (Jeremiah 23:5–6)

THE DIVINE NAME REVEALED IN THE MESSIAH

The passage opens with a messianic title we are now familiar with: "the righteous Branch." In both Isaiah and Zechariah, the Branch refers to the messianic King who will emerge from the line of David and rule with justice forever. But this prophecy adds a remarkable twist—this King is given the divine name: *YHVH Tsidkenu*—"The LORD is Our Righteousness."

To Jewish ears, this was thunderous. YHVH is the covenant name of Israel's God—the unpronounceable, ineffable name revealed to Moses at the burning bush. Yet this is the very name by which the future Davidic King will be called. This is not merely a title of honor or an association with divine authority. It is an identification. The coming King is not only from David's line—He is YHVH in human form.

RIGHTEOUSNESS IS A PERSON

The idea of God providing His people with righteousness is not new, but here, it is concentrated in a Person. This is not simply a king who will lead justly. The King is Righteousness itself. Even more shockingly, He bestows that righteousness upon His people. The name given to

ONE KING OVER JUDAH AND ISRAEL

Him mirrors what was once said of Jerusalem (Jer. 33:16), but here, the emphasis shifts to the Person of the King. He is not just the instrument of righteousness. He is righteousness personified.

This King's reign will bring about the salvation and the safety of both Israel and Judah. In Jeremiah's day, these two kingdoms were both shattered. Their security was gone, their leaders were corrupt, and their future seemed lost. But the Righteous Branch, as the restorer of David's Kingdom, would restore all that was broken. He would not merely restore the Kingdom of Judah, but He would unify both fallen Kingdoms.

GLOBAL REDEMPTION

This prophecy anticipates not just political and geographical restoration, but spiritual restoration under a divine King who reigns in justice. The good news of the Gospel has always been much more than a simple message concerning the spiritual salvation of one's soul. It is, and has always been, a comprehensive and holistic message concerning the restoration of all things. The restoration of the Kingdom of David is far more than just the restoration of the royal Jewish Monarchy. It is the restoration of the entire creation, the whole cosmos. The Throne of David, however, will always be the centerpiece of this restored planet. It will become the locus of global power, the launching pad for cosmic redemption.

This passage also draws a stark contrast between the failed shepherds of Israel—whom the Lord condemns earlier in the chapter—and the righteous reign of the coming Messiah. Not much different than so many corrupt politicians and even spiritual leaders in our day, the leaders of Jeremiah's day scattered the flock, neglected justice, and led the people into judgment. But the Righteous Branch will do just the opposite. He will gather the flock, shepherd them wisely, and rule in righteousness, *forever*.

LORD OF THE UNIVERSE

CHAPTER 17

THE **GOOD**
SHEPHERD

AMONG ALL OF THE MESSIANIC PROPHECIES THUS FAR, Ezekiel 34 may be the most pastoral. Here, the Lord speaks through Ezekiel to condemn the false shepherds of Israel—her corrupt kings, prophets, and priests:

> Then the word of the Lord came to me saying, "Son of man, prophesy against the shepherds of Israel. Prophesy and say to those shepherds, 'Thus says the Lord God, "Woe, shepherds of Israel who have been feeding themselves! Should not the shepherds feed the flock? You eat the fat and clothe yourselves with the wool, you slaughter the fat sheep without feeding the flock."'" (Ezekiel 34:1–3)

One can hear the Lord's great empathy and concern for the weak, the needy, and the exploited among His flock:

> "Those who are sickly you have not strengthened, the diseased you have not healed, the broken you have not bound up, the scattered you have not brought back, nor have you sought for the lost; but with force and with severity you have dominated them. They were scattered for lack of a shepherd, and they became food for every beast of the field and were scattered. My flock wandered through all the mountains and on every high hill; My flock was scattered over all the surface of the earth, and there was no one to search or seek for them." (Ezekiel 34:4–6)

ONE SHEPHERD

Then the Lord promises that in light of the failure of His representatives to care for His flock, He Himself will take on the role. He will personally shepherd His people.

> For thus says the Lord God, "Behold, I Myself will search for My sheep and seek them out. As a shepherd cares for his herd in the day when he is among his scattered sheep, so I will care for My sheep and will deliver them from all the places to which they were scattered on

a cloudy and gloomy day. I will bring them out from the peoples and gather them from the countries and bring them to their own land; and I will feed them on the mountains of Israel, by the streams, and in all the inhabited places of the land. I will feed them in a good pasture, and their grazing ground will be on the mountain heights of Israel. There they will lie down on good grazing ground and feed in rich pasture on the mountains of Israel. I will feed My flock and I will lead them to rest," declares the Lord God. "I will seek the lost, bring back the scattered, bind up the broken, and strengthen the sick; but the fat and the strong I will destroy. I will feed them with judgment." (Ezekiel 34:11–16)

In verse 23, we have the culmination of the prophecy:

"Then I will set over them one shepherd, My servant David, and he will feed them; he will feed them himself and be their shepherd." (Ezekiel 34:23)

Not only does the Lord express His compassionate shepherd's heart over His people, but in verse 23, we also see a stunning statement. For on the one hand, the Lord says, "I Myself will search for My sheep." But then, just a few verses later, He promises to set over them "one Shepherd, My servant David." So which is it? Is the Lord Himself the Shepherd, or is it the Davidic King?

The answer is both.

This prophecy once again deliberately interweaves the identities of YHVH and the Davidic King. The Shepherd who feeds and protects the flock is both God and His chosen human representative. Just as the divine name is applied to the Branch in Jeremiah, here the shepherding work of God is carried out through David's greater Son.

One can also hear echoes of Psalm 23, where David famously declares that, "The Lord is my Shepherd." The presence of the Good Shepherd is always accompanied by imagery rich with comfort: green

THE SHEPHERD KING

pastures, still waters, restoration, and guidance. Ezekiel, however, is not just speaking generally, but extends his vision into the eschatological Messianic Kingdom. At that time, the scattered sheep of Israel will not only be tended and fed—they will be regathered, healed, and unified under a single and eternal Shepherd-King.

ONE NATION, UNDER GOD, INDIVISIBLE

Later, in Ezekiel 37, the same theme intensifies. After the famous vision of the dry bones, the Lord promises to reunite the northern and southern kingdoms and restore them under One King:

> "My servant David will be king over them, and they will all have one Shepherd; and they will walk in My ordinances and keep My statutes and observe them. They will live on the land that I gave to Jacob My servant... and David My servant will be their prince forever." (Ezekiel 37:24–25)

The repetition is emphatic. One King. One Shepherd. One people. No longer divided and no longer scattered. This is a vision of restored Israel under her Messiah, all living in faithfulness.

> "They will live on the land that I gave to Jacob My servant, in which your fathers lived; and they will live on it, they, and their sons and their sons' sons, forever; and David My servant will be their prince forever. I will make a covenant of peace with them; it will be an everlasting covenant with them. And I will place them and multiply them, and will set My sanctuary in their midst forever. My dwelling place also will be with them; and I will be their God, and they will be My people. And the nations will know that I am the Lord who sanctifies Israel, when My sanctuary is in their midst forever." (Ezekiel 37:25–28)

Here, the Messianic Age is portrayed not only as a time of peace but also as a time of complete reunification. The Lord promises to restore His covenant with His people. This will not be a temporary covenant, but everlasting. Israel will then live in their land permanently. YHVH will be their God, and they will be His people. The Lord even promises to rebuild His temple during this time.

JESUS IS THE GOOD SHEPHERD

In the New Testament, Jesus applies this vision to Himself, making it abundantly clear how He viewed Himself. He is both YHVH and the Davidic Son. One can hear one of the disciples asking, "Jesus, who are you?" And then He responds:

> "I am the good shepherd; the good shepherd lays down His life for the sheep. He who is a hired hand, and not a shepherd, who is not the owner of the sheep, sees the wolf coming, and leaves the sheep and flees, and the wolf snatches them and scatters them. He flees because he is a hired hand and is not concerned about the sheep. I am the good shepherd, and I know My own and My own know Me, even as the Father knows Me and I know the Father; and I lay down My life for the sheep." (John 10:11–15)

Jesus is the Good Shepherd who lays down His life for the sheep, who will gather them into one flock, and lead them into eternal life. The One Shepherd of Ezekiel becomes the cornerstone of New Testament Christology. He is the King and Priest who will restore the throne and kingdom of David.

THE GOOD SHEPHERD

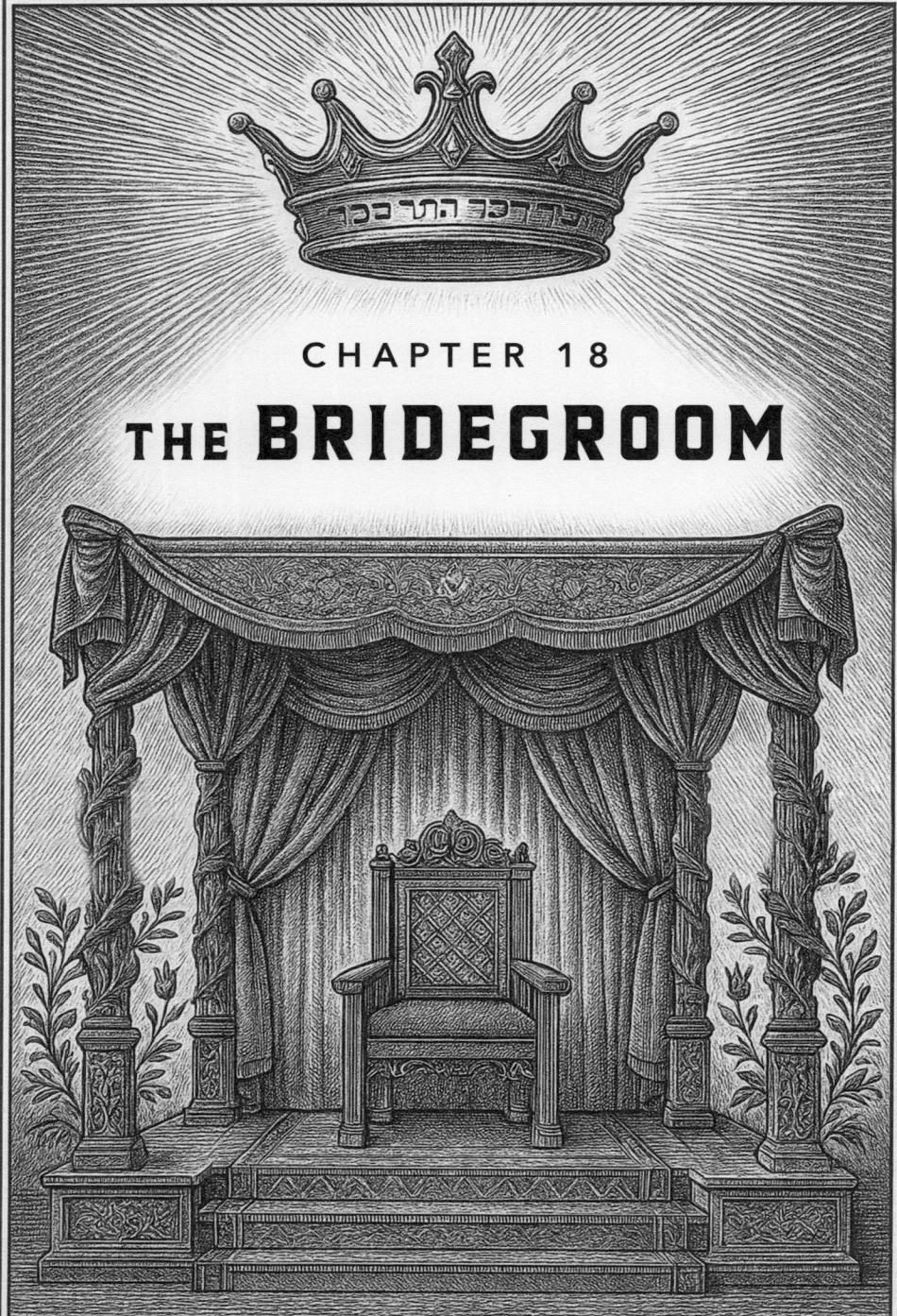

CHAPTER 18

the BRIDEGROOM

ANOTHER BEAUTIFUL MESSIANIC PROPHECY is found in Psalm 45. Here, the Messiah is celebrated both as an eternal king and a radiant bridegroom, intermixing the imagery of beauty, warfare, divine enthronement, and marital joy—all into one stunning and sublime portrait.

Though often viewed merely as a royal wedding psalm, the structure, language, and placement of Psalm 45 within the Psalter reveal something far more profound. The psalm envisions something much greater than a simple historic, royal wedding. It envisions the glories of the coming Messianic King, who is the Divine Bridegroom of Israel. As the psalmist begins to write, we can feel his eager anticipation for what is to follow:

> My heart overflows with a good theme; I address my verses to the King; My tongue is the pen of a ready writer. You are fairer than the sons of men; Grace is poured upon Your lips; Therefore God has blessed You forever. (Psalm 45:1–2)

FROM LONGING TO CELEBRATION

The placement of this psalm within the Psalter—the Book of Psalms— helps us to understand how it was viewed in ancient times. Book II of the Psalms (Psalms 42–49) begins with a three-part lament (Psalms 42–44). These three psalms are defined by sorrow over two things: the loss of God's presence and Israel's ongoing exile. Israel longs to return to their homeland and to experience the presence of God once again. They are crying out from exile and asking why it feels as though God has abandoned them. They remember the days of Temple worship and plead for its restoration.

Then Psalm 45 is the turning point—a transition from longing into a royal celebration. Instead of lament, now the Messiah emerges in radiant beauty, girded with a sword, riding forth with both majesty and humility.

THE BRIDEGROOM WARRIOR

Gird Your sword on Your thigh, O Mighty One, In Your splendor and Your majesty! And in Your majesty ride on victoriously, For the cause of truth and meekness and righteousness; Let Your right hand teach You awesome things. Your arrows are sharp; The peoples fall under You; Your arrows are in the heart of the King's enemies. (Psalm 45:3–5)

As the psalm continues, the King defeats Israel's enemies and establishes His eternal throne. Then, the bride is led into the palace with joy.

THE IDENTITY OF THE KING

Psalm 45 directly addresses the King as God:

Your throne, O God, is forever and ever; A scepter of uprightness is the scepter of Your kingdom. You have loved righteousness and hated wickedness; Therefore God, Your God, has anointed You With the oil of joy above Your fellows. (Psalm 45:6–7)

Despite centuries of interpreters trying to soften this claim, the plain reading stands firm. No earthly king in Israel's history ever received such divine accolades. He is praised forever. He is bowed to. His name is remembered across generations. These are honors reserved for God alone—not only throughout the Psalms, but throughout the whole Bible.

But while this King is indeed divine, He is also portrayed as human. He rides into battle. He receives a bride. He is anointed and rejoices in the palace. This psalm joins others like Psalms 2, 72, and 110 in revealing the Messiah as the mysterious figure who is both God and man—the true Son of David and yet David's Lord.

Descriptions of the extravagance of the royal wedding celebrations continue:

"All Your garments are fragrant with myrrh and aloes and cassia; Out of ivory palaces stringed instruments have made You glad." (Psalm 45:8)

THE WEDDING

THE IDENTITY OF THE BRIDE

The bride, adorned and radiant, represents Israel—but even more broadly, the faithful from every nation. When we understand the progressive storyline unfolding in these psalms, then we can hear the longings of this bride, as voiced earlier: *"When shall I come and appear before God?"* (Psalm 42:2). Here, at last, she arrives, decked out in gold. The psalmist captures her wedding day splendor:

"At Your right hand stands the queen in gold from Ophir." (Psalm 45:9)

Similar wedding imagery echoes throughout the prophecies of Hosea, Isaiah, and Ezekiel, where Israel's restoration is described as a renewed marriage. God, the Divine Husband, woos His unfaithful bride back into His arms, washes her, and restores her with His everlasting love.

THE BATTLEFIELD AND THE PALACE

Psalm 45 describes two distinct settings: the battlefield and the palace. The Messiah first appears as a warrior-king, riding out in truth and righteousness to defeat evil. Then, He is enthroned, receiving glory, worship, and a bride inside His palace. These two scenes directly correspond to Israel's two great yearnings in Psalms 42–44. In Psalm 44, Israel laments that God no longer marches out with their armies. Then, in Psalm 45, the King straps on His sword and rides forth. In Psalms 42 and 43, Israel longs to be led into God's dwelling place. In Psalm 45, the bride is finally led in with joy to the King's palace. The Divine Warrior thus restores all that had been lost. The King restores both "peace through victory" and the very presence of God with His people.

MESSIANIC ECHOES

Psalm 45 also synchronizes with earlier Messianic promises, making it clear that the King here is indeed the Promised One. Like Genesis 49, the King is praised by His brothers and bowed down to by all peoples. Like 2 Samuel 7, He sits on an eternal throne. Like Isaiah 9, He is the

Mighty God who rules with righteousness. This is not a generic royal psalm—it contains the very heartbeat of Israel's hope.

JESUS THE BRIDEGROOM

If one desires to understand the overarching biblical narrative, then one must recognize that the covenant made between YHVH and Israel at Mount Sinai was a wedding, or more specifically, a betrothal ceremony. It is for this reason that after Sinai, the Lord repeatedly refers to Himself as Israel's husband:

> "For your husband is your Maker, Whose name is the Lord of hosts; And your Redeemer is the Holy One of Israel, Who is called the God of all the earth. For the Lord has called you, Like a wife forsaken and grieved in spirit, Even like a wife of one's youth when she is rejected," Says your God. "For a brief moment I forsook you, But with great compassion I will gather you. In an outburst of anger I hid My face from you for a moment, But with everlasting lovingkindness I will have compassion on you," Says the Lord your Redeemer. (Isaiah 54:5–8)

There is a mystery hidden in plain sight that we cannot miss here. In the New Testament, when Jesus repeatedly identifies Himself as the Bridegroom (Matthew 9:15; John 3:29), He was in fact, making a straightforward claim, in effect, saying, "I am the Bridegroom God of Mount Sinai—the Warrior, the King, and the Bridegroom of Psalm 45."

The apostles also pick up this theme, portraying the Church as the Lord's bride (Ephesians 5:25–32; Revelation 21:2). Psalm 45 anticipates all of this. It is the song of the Messiah who conquers, reigns, and marries His people with everlasting joy. The psalm closes with the beautiful promise:

> "I will cause Your name to be remembered in all generations; Therefore the peoples will give You thanks forever and ever." (v. 17)

The King will forever be praised—not only by Israel but by a vast multitude from every tongue, tribe, people, and nation.

THE BRIDEGROOM AND QUEEN IN GOLD

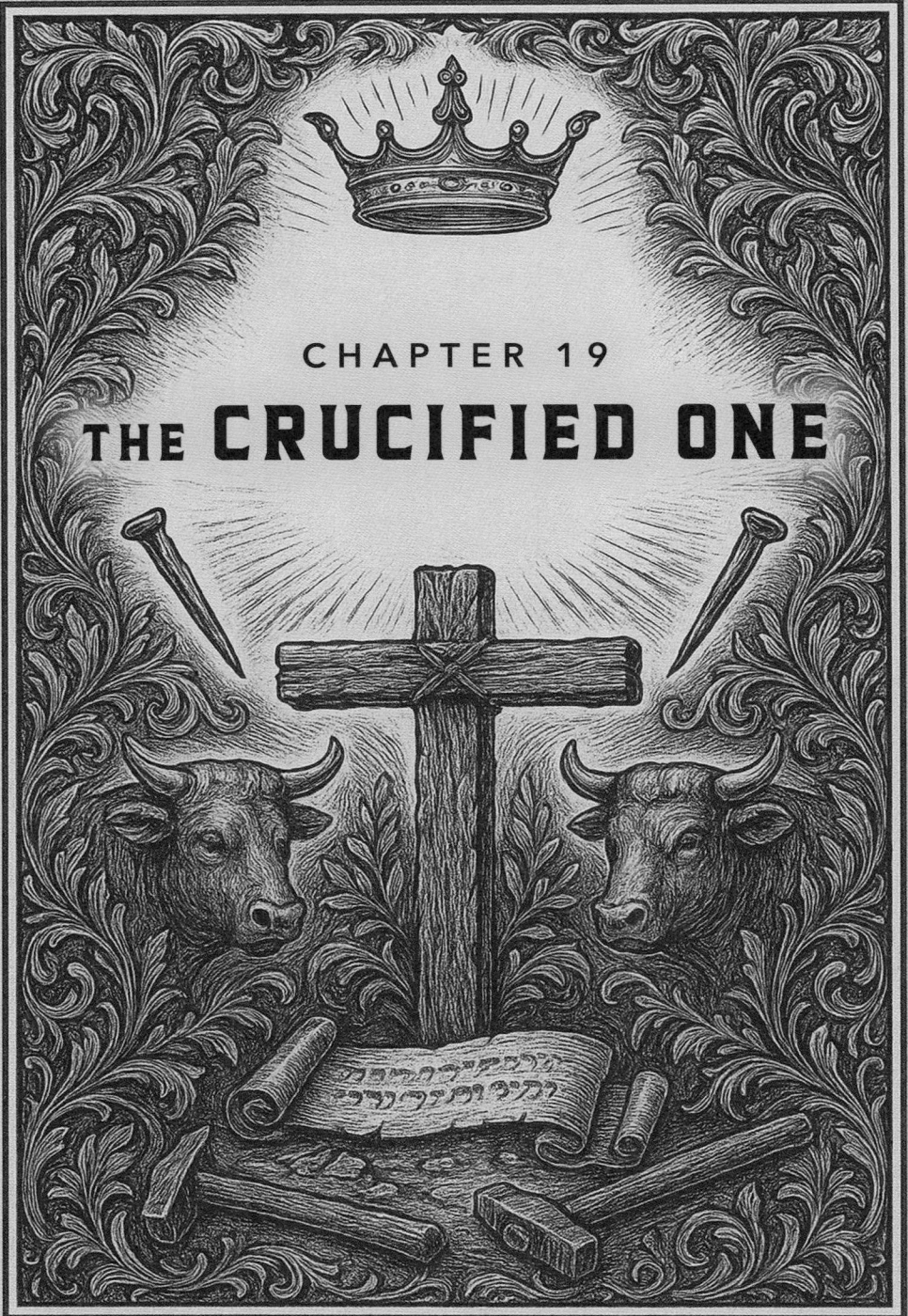

CHAPTER 19

THE CRUCIFIED ONE

OVER THE YEARS, I've spent a considerable amount of time discussing the Gospel with Muslims. One of their most common objections to Jesus being God is His cry while on the cross in which He shouts, *"Eli Eli Lama Sabachthani,"* which means, "My God, my God, why have you forsaken me?" On the surface, this may seem to have some merit. How could Jesus be all-knowing but still be shocked, and seemingly even dismayed or confused as to what was happening to Him? But this is a tragic misunderstanding of Jesus' words in their proper context.

The truth is that when Jesus shouted these words as He hung there on the cross, He was not panicking. He was not confused or questioning God. Quite to the contrary, even in His agony, He was in control enough to continue to teach those who had ears to hear. Jesus was making one of the most amazing prophetic declarations of His entire ministry. He was quoting the opening line of Psalm 22—word for word—from memory. In the Jewish world of His day, quoting the first line of a passage was a way of referencing the entire psalm. In that moment, Jesus was declaring that Psalm 22 was about Him. He was telling His disciples—and anyone else watching—that what was happening was not a mistake. It was prophecy being fulfilled right before their eyes.

As Jesus hung there on the cross, with thick Roman nails having been driven through both His hands and feet, He was calling His disciples' minds to the words of the psalmist:

> Many bulls have surrounded me; For dogs have surrounded me; A band of evildoers has encompassed me; They pierced my hands and my feet. (v. 16)

Jesus was saying: "Behold, I am He." Jesus was declaring to every Jew who knew his Bible who was present that His crucifixion was not the failure of God's plan, but the very center of it. He was not a helpless victim; He is the prophesied suffering King of Psalm 22.

PSALM 22 IN CONTEXT

Psalm 22 doesn't stand alone. It's part of a carefully placed sequence in the Psalter that began in Psalms 1–2 with a royal figure called the "Anointed One." Despite being rejected by the raging Gentile nations, this figure is promised global dominion. Building on this theme, Psalm 21 speaks of a king who rejoices in God's salvation. Then suddenly, Psalm 22 opens with this same king crying out in abandonment: *"My God, My God, why have You forsaken Me?"* What happened?

Psalm 22 tells the story of the suffering and death of this royal figure—the Messianic King. He is scorned, surrounded by enemies, physically tortured, and ultimately brought to the "dust of death." His hands and feet are pierced. His bones are exposed. His clothes are divided up by his executioners. This is undeniably describing crucifixion—laid out in precise detail hundreds of years before it was invented.

As stunning as this is, the psalm does not end with death. It ends with victory! In verse 21, everything turns. God answers the cries of His suffering King. Suddenly, we hear the voice of resurrection. The King, once despised and forsaken, is now alive and praising God amongst the great congregation. His deliverance sparks worship not only in Israel but also among the nations. Even the dead and future generations are praising Him! He is the One through whom the entire earth returns to the Lord. Psalm 22 is unquestionably one of the most amazingly prophetic psalms imaginable.

FROM SUFFERING TO RESURRECTION

The flow of Psalm 22 moves from rejection to resurrection. This is precisely how the apostles understood and would later portray the story of Jesus. He was the King who suffered, the Servant who was pierced, and the Son who rose from the dead. The final line of the psalm states:

> "They will come and will declare His righteousness to a people who will be born, that He has performed it." (Psalm 22:31)

PSALM 22

One translation reads: "He has done it"—a phrase that instantly reminds us of Jesus' last words on the cross: "*It is finished.*"

Adding to the beauty of this prophetic psalm, we note that it flows directly into Psalm 23. After being pierced, after suffering betrayal, crucifixion, and death—after walking through the valley of the shadow of death—the King is now led beside still waters. The Shepherd King, who once lay dying, is now alive and guiding others to life. Then, in Psalm 24, the King enters Zion as the King of Glory. There is purpose in the arrangement of the Psalter—they tell the story of redemption. They describe and outline the Messiah's journey from suffering to exaltation, from crucifixion to enthronement.

SUFFERING BEFORE GLORY

Psalm 22 is an open window through which to view redemptive history. The Messiah suffers not as a victim of chance but as the fulfillment of God's perfect unfolding plan. It is through His death that God's promise to Abraham will be fulfilled—that all nations would be blessed through his seed. The language of the Abrahamic covenant is echoed explicitly throughout the final verses of Psalm 22:

> "All the ends of the earth will remember and turn to the Lord, And all the families of the nations will worship before You." (v. 27)

Psalm 22 articulates the gospel of salvation, written in poetic form. A King crushed, crucified, raised to everlasting life, and offering life to all peoples from every nation, even to the very ends of the earth.

CHAPTER 20

THE SUFFERING SERVANT

AS THE GENESIS 3:15 "SEED" PROPHECY INDICATED, before Satan would be crushed by the Promised One, he would manage to get off one "strike" at his victor's heel. Precisely what that meant, however, was not made clear at the time. Although many details concerning the nature and mission of the Messiah would eventually emerge with great clarity, others remained mysterious. He is the King who will "strike the earth with the rod of His mouth," yet He is also the one who is bruised. This presents a paradox. Further, while He is born of a woman, He is also preexistent, eternal, and even called Mighty God. Some passages speak of Him coming to bring deliverance; others talk of YHVH Himself coming to save. Those awaiting the Messiah no doubt wrestled with some of these tensions. The prophecies after Genesis 3:15 primarily emphasized the Messiah's strength, victory, and kingship, but the details of His wounding remained veiled until Psalm 22. It is in the prophecies of Isaiah that the full nature of the Messiah's suffering would become abundantly clear.

THE SERVANT SONGS

Within the book of Isaiah, there are four prophetic songs where the Messiah is referred to as "the Servant." These passages provide a groundbreaking revelation concerning His suffering. With masterful suspense, Isaiah unveils these truths gradually, culminating in the explosive clarity of chapters 52 and 53. The Servant Songs mark a pivotal shift in messianic prophecy.

THE FIRST SERVANT SONG (ISAIAH 42)

The first Servant Song begins:

> "Behold, My Servant, whom I uphold; My chosen one in whom My soul delights. I have put My Spirit upon Him; He will bring forth justice to the nations" (Isaiah 42:1).

BOUND IN SORROW

YHVH declares that He will place His Spirit upon this Servant. The Servant will bring justice not only to Israel but to the nations (vv. 3–4). God says to Him, "I will appoint You as a covenant to the people, as a light to the nations" (v. 6). The Abrahamic, Mosaic, and Davidic covenants were all given to Israel but anticipated blessing the Gentiles as well. Here, a new covenant is mentioned. Unlike any of the previous covenants, however, this one is embodied in the Servant Himself. He doesn't merely bring a covenant; He Himself is the covenant. This is a critical point because only YHVH can make or embody such a covenant. Lastly, the beautiful purpose of the Servant's ministry is to "open blind eyes, to bring out prisoners from the dungeon and those who dwell in darkness from the prison" (v. 7).

THE SECOND SERVANT SONG (ISAIAH 49)

In this song, the Servant is called "Israel" (v. 3). This is not a contradiction. As with references to the Messiah as "David," this title portrays Him as the perfect representative of Israel, accomplishing all that the nation could not. His mission is to restore the tribes of Jacob and bring salvation to the ends of the earth (v. 6). All of these are things that only the Messiah can do.

Then comes a startling shift: the Servant is "despised... abhorred by the nation" (v. 7). The ministry of the Messiah will not come without significant detractors and hate. Despite all of this rejection, He will ultimately be vindicated: "Kings will see and arise, Princes will also bow down, Because of the Lord who is faithful" (v. 7). Once more, He is called a covenant to the people, and this time with the specific purpose of restoring Israel's inheritance of the land (v. 8). Sadly, it is pretty common among many Christians today to ignore texts such as this one and to wrongly claim that the New Covenant has nothing to do with the promised land. But Isaiah ties the New Covenant directly to the promised land that the Messiah will secure. The result will be joy and comfort for all who are afflicted (v. 13).

THE SUFFERING SERVANT

THE THIRD SERVANT SONG (ISAIAH 50)

Here, in the third Servant Song, the theme of suffering deepens. The Servant says:

> "I gave My back to those who strike Me, And My cheeks to those who pluck out the beard; I did not cover My face from humiliation and spitting" (v. 6).

Though obedient and innocent, He is subjected to brutal treatment. Yet He remains steadfast: "I have set My face like flint... He who vindicates Me is near" (vv. 7–8). The Messiah accepts this suffering willingly—a costly obedience that would bring about His exaltation.

THE FOURTH SERVANT SONG (ISAIAH 52:13-53:12)

Each Servant Song progressively opens the curtain wider. As such, the final song is truly breathtaking in its depth. One scholar compares reading this section to the high priest moving from the Holy Place into the Holy of Holies. It begins triumphantly: "Behold, My servant will prosper, He will be high and lifted up and greatly exalted" (52:13). This is language most often reserved for YHVH Himself. But the following verse shifts rather violently: "His appearance was marred more than any man" (v. 14). Then again, the scene shifts: "He shall startle many nations; kings shall be silenced because of Him" (v. 15). The paradox of humiliation and exaltation is restated. Then Isaiah asks a poignant question: "Who has believed our message? And to whom has the arm of the Lord been revealed?" (53:1). This term is unmistakably rooted in the story of the exodus. "The arm of the Lord," "the hand of the Lord," or "a mighty and outstretched arm" all carry the same connotations. When the Lord led Israel out of Egypt, it was as though He reached down from heaven to accomplish His purposes and do mighty miracles on the earth below. Any biblically literate Jew who hears this term would immediately think of the exodus and God's most powerful acts in all of redemptive history (see Ex 6:6; Dt 5:15; 7:19). To appeal to

God to reveal His arm is to appeal to God to repeat what He did when He led Israel out of Egypt. Thus, when Isaiah interceded for Israel's deliverance from oppression in his day, he cried out: "Awake, awake, put on strength, O arm of the Lord. Awake as in the days of old, the generations of long ago" (Is 51:9).

Thus, when chapter 53 begins by mentioning the arm of the Lord, it comes with the full expectation that what will come next is the destruction of Israel's enemies. That, however, is not at all what we find—just the opposite. The script is completely flipped. Instead, Isaiah shocks his audience by elaborating on the suffering of the Servant with a depth that far surpasses any of the previous songs. It begins with His birth and childhood:

> "And like a root out of parched ground; He has no stately form or majesty That we should look upon Him, Nor appearance that we should be attracted to Him. He was despised and forsaken of men, A man of sorrows and acquainted with grief; And like one from whom men hide their face He was despised, and we did not esteem Him" (Isaiah 53:2–3).

The words "pierced" and "crushed" are usually associated with fatal blows. In the same way that God had "pierced the dragon" (Isa 51:9), now it is the Messiah who is pierced. It is a complete script flip: The one who was to crush Satan is Himself crushed! Yet, through this suffering comes new life: "By His scourging we are healed" (v. 5). Isaiah then adds: "The Lord has caused the iniquity of us all to fall on Him" (v. 6). This is not a failure of God's protection—this was God's will. The Servant submits silently, "like a lamb led to slaughter" (v. 7). He is "cut off from the land of the living" for the sins of others (v. 8). This is unmistakably a prophecy of violent death in which He dies for the very people who killed Him.

Yet after death comes a shocking twist: "His grave was assigned with wicked men, Yet He was with a rich man in His death" (v. 9). This highly specific prophecy would be fulfilled to the letter. It defies the possibility of manipulation. And it marks the beginning of His vindication. Then the climax: "The Lord was pleased to crush Him... He will render Himself as a guilt offering... He will see His offspring, prolong His days" (v. 10). The Servant's death is framed as a sacrificial offering (Hebrew: 'asham), used in temple rituals for atonement. By bearing our sin, He justifies many. Despite His death, He will live again, share the spoils of victory, and intercede on behalf of sinners (vv. 11–12). Only God could orchestrate such a prophecy, and only the true Messiah could fulfill it.

These Servant Songs were central to first-century Jewish messianic expectations. They saw in these texts the portrait of a mysterious figure: divine, yet despised; exalted, yet pierced; rejected, yet victorious. Many would only recognize Him after His resurrection. Others still wait to see Him when He comes again in power.

The Suffering Servant is the key to unlocking the paradoxes of messianic prophecy. Here is the bruised heel, the guilt offering, the crucified one, but also the victorious King. Isaiah foresaw His suffering, death, burial, resurrection, and his ultimate reign. It is through Him that God's covenant is fulfilled, the nations are healed, and the curse is reversed. Only in the Suffering Servant do the promises of Scripture find their complete, breathtaking fulfillment.

ZECHARIAH AND THE PIERCED LORD

Other prophets hinted at the Messiah's suffering, but none with the precision of Isaiah. Zechariah, writing later, clearly draws on Isaiah's Servant imagery. In Zechariah 12, the Lord declares: "They will look on Me whom they have pierced; and they will mourn for Him" (v. 10). YHVH says that Israel will recognize Him as the One they pierced. They will weep with the grief of realizing that their long-awaited King, their Savior, was the One they had rejected. Isaiah described the atonement; Zechariah describes the national moment of recognition and repentance.

CHAPTER 21

THE DESERT MARCHER

MANY YEARS AFTER Moses issued his final blessing, after prophesying about YHVH, the Cloud Rider, other prophets would build upon the foundation Moses had laid. In the pages of Isaiah and Habakkuk, in particular, all the threads converge. The Skull Crusher of Eden and the Cloud Rider of Sinai are revealed to be one and the same.

TREADING THE WINEPRESS

Isaiah 63 opens with a dramatic vision. Isaiah is in Jerusalem, looking to the south. He sees a majestic figure marching toward him. Astonished at what he sees, he asks:

> "Who is this who comes from Edom, With garments of glowing colors from Bozrah, This One who is majestic in His apparel, Marching in the greatness of His strength?" (Isaiah 63:1)

Isaiah beholds a resolute warrior, coming through the land of Edom—Israel's ancient enemy to the southeast. His garments are vivid red. He is majestic, radiant, and terrifying. Then He speaks: "It is I who speak in righteousness, mighty to save" (v. 1b). Still perplexed as to why this majestic figure's robes are so vivid and red, Isaiah asks:

> "Why is Your apparel red, And Your garments like one who treads in the wine press?" (v. 2)

The answer is shocking:

> "I have trodden the wine trough alone, And from the peoples there was no one with Me. I also trod them in My anger And trampled them in My wrath; And their lifeblood is sprinkled on My garments, And I stained all My clothes." (v. 3)

This is judgment in its most raw and violent form. The Lord is soaked in the blood of His enemies. The wrath of God is on full display.

ISAIAH BEHOLDS THE DESERT MARCHER

Why has He taken such extreme measures? The answer can only be explained in light of the horror of all that has been inflicted against the people of God. After millennia of Satanic persecution and rage being directed against the saints, the Lord declares why He is soaked in blood: "For the day of vengeance was in My heart, and My year of redemption has come" (v. 4). These two realities are not in tension. Vengeance and redemption are always intertwined. In biblical thought, the judgment of the wicked is always the deliverance of the righteous. The death of the arrogant means the liberation of the oppressed. This One who marches through the desert is the divine King who is rescuing His people and reclaiming His dominion.

HABAKKUK'S VISION

Habakkuk 3 gives us a similar striking vision. Sounding almost identical to the blessings of Moses in Deuteronomy 33, Habakkuk describes what he sees:

> "God comes from Teman, And the Holy One from Mount Paran. His splendor covers the heavens, And the earth is full of His praise. His radiance is like the sunlight; He has rays flashing from His hand, And there is the hiding of His power." (Habakkuk 3:3–4)

This is not just poetic language. This is real geography. Mount Paran is a mountain that sits along the border of northwest Saudi Arabia and the Kingdom of Jordan. Teman refers to the south. Like Enoch, Moses, or Isaiah before him, Habakkuk similarly describes the God of Sinai marching through the deserts of the exodus, making His way toward Zion. This is the greater Exodus, the final march:

> "You marched through the earth in indignation; You trampled the nations in anger. You went forth for the salvation of Your people, For the salvation of Your anointed." (v. 12)

CRUSHING THE HEAD OF THE HOUSE OF EVIL

Then, we are brought back to Genesis 3:15. Once again, the head of the serpent is struck. The final Antichrist, like Pharaoh, Sisera, and Goliath before him, will receive the final crushing death blow to his head:

"You struck the head of the house of evil To lay him open from thigh to neck." (v. 13)

Here, all of the visions and motifs come together: the Skull Crusher of Genesis 3:15 and the Cloud Rider of Deuteronomy 33 are one and the same. It is all one single glorious story.

PSALM 68: THE PROCESSION OF GOD

Throughout the exodus journey, whenever the pillar of cloud would move forward, the people of Israel would pack up their tents and belongings and prepare to travel. As they began the next leg of their journey, the priests would grasp the rods that ran through the rings on the side of the ark. As they lifted it, Moses would pray this prayer: "Let God arise, let His enemies be scattered" (v. 1). Thus, beginning with the prayer of Moses, Psalm 68 amplifies the same themes as those found in Isaiah or Habakkuk. There, the prayer is essentially a request for God to arise from His throne in heaven and come down to defeat His enemies. It is the Maranatha cry, if you will, of the Old Testament. "Oh Lord, come down and save us!"

Psalm 68 then recounts God's victorious march from Sinai into the promised land. This is no mere retrospective, however. Once more, it is prophecy wearing the clothes of history. The psalmist sees God rising again:

"O God, when You went forth before Your people, When You marched through the wilderness, Selah. The earth quaked; The heavens also dropped rain at the presence of God; Sinai itself quaked at the presence of God, the God of Israel." (vv. 7–8)

As the psalm unfolds, the language grows more triumphant:

"The Lord gives the command; The women who proclaim the good news are a great host... Kings of armies flee, they flee, And she who remains at home will divide the spoil." (vv. 11–12)

The women present, who are part of the grand procession, are shouting aloud as the armies of the Antichrist are fleeing from before the majestic One. The source of their terror is clear:

"They have seen Your procession, O God, The procession of my God, my King, into the sanctuary. The singers went on, the musicians after them, In the midst of the maidens beating tambourines." (vv. 24–25)

The multi-faceted vibrancy of this vision is marvelous. Not only is the warrior victoriously marching through the desert, delivering prisoners, with His face set like flint toward Jerusalem, but it also describes the worshippers, singers, and musicians both leading and following after the procession. It is a bloody war movie, but also a musical. Like the most majestic military parade that has ever been, the procession of God toward the sanctuary may be one of the richest and exhilarating visions in all of Scripture.

We return to another majestic statement:

"You have ascended on high, You have led captive Your captives; You have received gifts among men, Even among the rebellious also, that the Lord God may dwell there." (v. 18)

This march has an end goal, a destination. It culminates with His enthronement. The Desert Marcher becomes the King. The captives are liberated. The rebellious are judged. Now God takes up His dwelling among His people.

THE GLORIOUS PROCESSION

DIVINE AND HUMAN: TWO COMINGS FORETOLD

A remarkable truth emerges from these texts: long before the New Testament, the concept of two comings is already established. In Isaiah 63, Habakkuk 3, and Psalm 68, a figure who is both divine and human is revealed. He is both the human seed of Eve, Abraham, and David, and He is YHVH, the majestic Cloud Rider. He must be naturally born as a human, but also someday come back from heaven as God Almighty. This is what the Old Testament teaches about the coming Messiah. Long before the New Testament, the prophets saw Him coming twice: first to suffer, then to judge and reign forever. The first time, He comes, born of a woman, meek and lowly, riding a donkey. The second time, He comes as the Cloud Rider, the Desert Marcher, thundering from heaven to save His people.

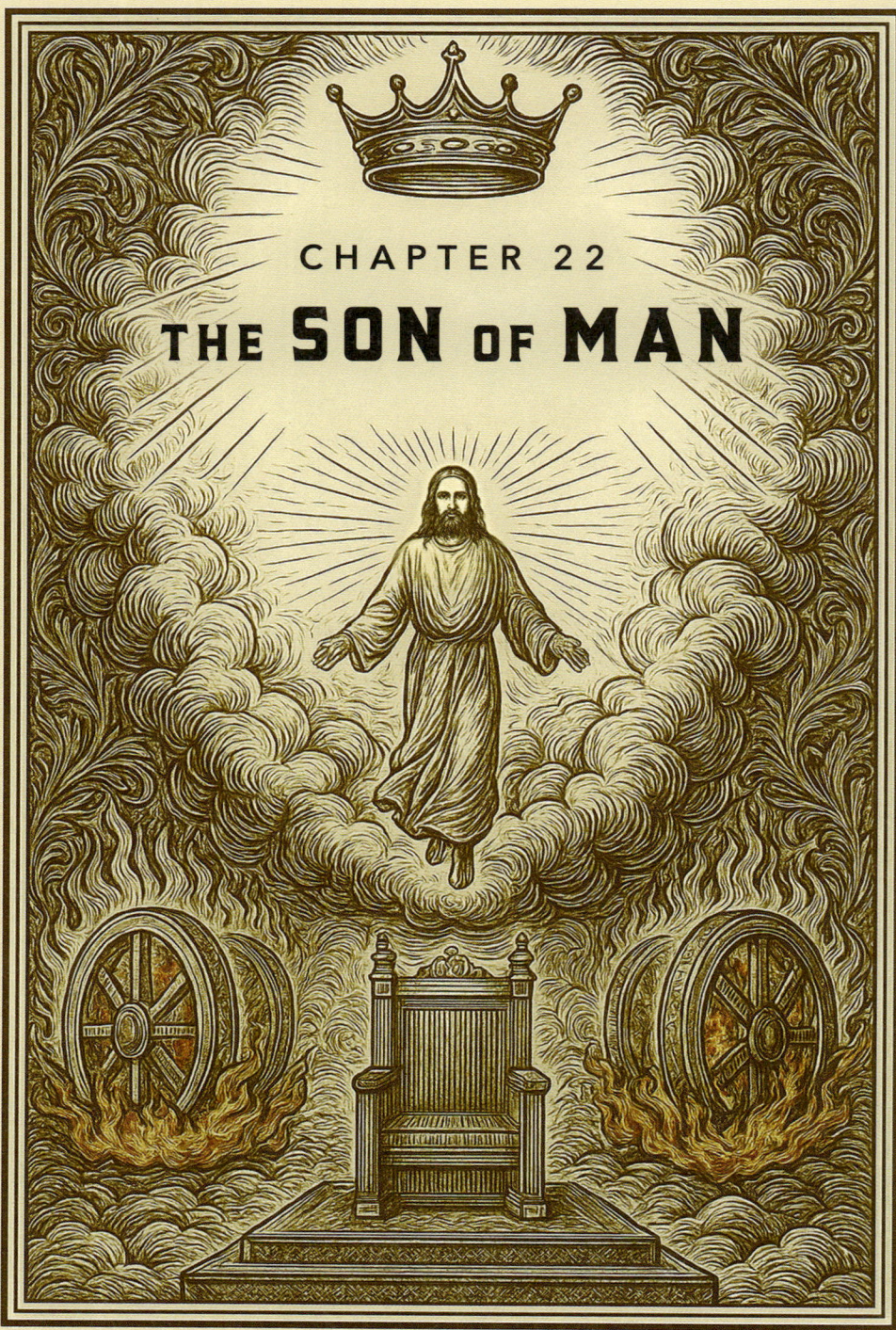

CHAPTER 22

THE SON OF MAN

ABOUT A HUNDRED YEARS after Isaiah warned Judah of coming judgment, his prophecies were fulfilled. The Babylonians invaded, conquered the kingdom, and exiled its people. While in Babylon, the prophet Daniel received profound revelations concerning the Messiah. Among these, Daniel 7 stands as one of the greatest capstones among the many messianic prophecies in the Bible—it is a vision of the Messiah's ultimate victory and His enthronement as King.

DANIEL'S VISION OF THE BEASTS AND THE COURTROOM

Daniel's vision begins with four beasts rising from the sea—symbolic of four successive Gentile empires empowered by Satan. Each oppresses the people of God. The fourth beast is especially terrifying and represents the final satanic empire, led by the Antichrist, to be destroyed at the return of Jesus. This vision spans redemptive history—from the rise of these empires to the end of the age and the transition into the Messianic Kingdom.

After seeing the beasts, Daniel witnesses a heavenly courtroom scene:

> "I kept looking Until thrones were set up, And the Ancient of Days took His seat; His vesture was like white snow And the hair of His head like pure wool. His throne was ablaze with flames, Its wheels were a burning fire. A river of fire was flowing And coming out from before Him; Thousands upon thousands were attending Him, And myriads upon myriads were standing before Him; The court sat, And the books were opened." (Daniel 7:9–10)

Daniel sees multiple thrones, only one of which is occupied by the "Ancient of Days." He is described as having a human form, sitting down, with clothing and hair both brilliant white. The throne itself is blazing with fire. It also has fiery wheels, indicating that the throne of God is not a stationary seat, but a chariot-throne (Ezek. 1:15–23; Exod. 14:25; Nah. 3:2). A river of fire pours forth from the throne as myriads of heavenly beings stand before Him. Books are opened in preparation for divine judgment against the kingdom of the Antichrist. Then, another distinctly human figure appears:

> "I kept looking in the night visions, And behold, with the clouds of heaven One like a Son of Man was coming, And He came up to the Ancient of Days And was presented before Him. And to Him was given dominion, Glory and a kingdom, That all the peoples, nations and men of every language Might serve Him. His dominion is an everlasting dominion Which will not pass away; And His kingdom is one Which will not be destroyed." (Daniel 7:13–14)

This astonishing Old Testament messianic vision includes several key motifs: the Cloud Rider, the Son of Man, the thrones, and the divine identity of the Messiah.

THE DIVINE CLOUD RIDER

The figure comes "with the clouds of heaven"—a powerful image of divine presence. Throughout Scripture, clouds signify God's manifest presence. God descended in a cloud on Sinai (Ex. 24:16), filled the tabernacle and temple with His glory-cloud (Ex. 40:34; 1 Kings 8:10–13), and is described as "riding on the clouds" (Deut. 33:26; Ps. 68:32–33; 104:3). Only YHVH rides the clouds.

So when Daniel sees "one like a Son of Man" riding the clouds, he is deliberately portraying a human figure in the role of YHVH Himself. The phrase "Son of Man" indicates that he is in human form. Thus, this is a divine-human figure. He is not the Ancient of Days, but He is indeed YHVH God Almighty, nonetheless—a clear validation of Christian doctrine.

JESUS, THE SON OF MAN

Jesus was intimately familiar with this prophecy and frequently identified Himself with its central figure in this vision:

COMING OF THE SON OF MAN

"Truly I say to you, that you who have followed Me, in the regeneration when the Son of Man will sit on His glorious throne, you also shall sit upon twelve thrones, judging the twelve tribes of Israel." (Matthew 19:28)

"Then the sign of the Son of Man will appear in the sky, and then all the tribes of the earth will mourn, and they will see the Son of Man coming on the clouds of the sky with power and great glory." (Matthew 24:30)

By the time of Daniel's vision on the journey of unfolding the biblical narrative, the two threads of revelation—the thread of the Snake Crusher, the human Seed of Eve, and the thread of the Divine Cloud Rider who comes from heaven to save—these two threads are so integrally intertwined that it is impossible to separate them. Furthermore, these motifs are also intertwined with numerous other messianic prophecies, creating a vividly vibrant vision that describes both the identity and mission of the Promised One. In the first century, Jewish expectations of the coming Messiah had thoroughly combined all of these themes (cf. Jude 14–15).

Further proving that this King is divine, we note that His throne will be "established forever." This is a near-direct quote from God's promise in the Davidic Covenant (2 Sam. 7:13). Of course, to rule forever, He must live forever. He will enjoy "everlasting dominion" (v. 14). Adam was given a divine mandate to exercise dominion over the earth, but he failed. The Son of Man will exercise perfect dominion forever. The Son of Man is thus the second or greater Adam, fulfilling everything that the imperfect first Adam could not accomplish.

THRONES

Daniel sees multiple thrones. Who are they for? Some have suggested angels; others see a connection to the heavenly council in Revelation 4–5. Perhaps the best explanation is that Daniel was seeing the same thing David saw in Psalm 110:

"YHVH said to my Lord, 'Sit at My right hand until I make Your enemies a footstool for Your feet.'"

Jesus referenced this very passage during His trial:

"Hereafter you will see the Son of Man sitting at the right hand of Power, and coming on the clouds of heaven." (Matthew 26:64)

Though the high priest was condemning Him, Jesus warned that one day he would witness His exaltation and return. Jesus now sits enthroned at the Father's right hand, awaiting the day when He will return and take His seat on His glorious throne—the throne of David, on Mount Zion (Matt. 19:28; 25:31; Heb. 10:13).

The throne of David has not yet been restored. Jesus is not currently reigning from David's throne, here on earth. The final beast has not yet been destroyed. That day, however, is rapidly approaching.

THE SON OF MAN: THE MOST HIGH

Strikingly, in Daniel 7:27, the same dominion and worship given to the Son of Man in verse 14 are now ascribed to "the Most High." The Son of Man and the Most High are not separate beings, but two titles for the same figure—the Messiah.

CONCLUSION: THE CAPSTONE OF MESSIANIC REVELATION

"Son of Man" is the title Jesus used for Himself more than any other— over 80 times in the Gospels. Why? Because in using it, He was directly identifying Himself with Daniel 7's divine figure. This prophecy draws together all the threads we have followed: the Seed of the woman, the royal Son of David, the divine Cloud Rider.

All of these factors together lead us to conclude that the Son of Man in Daniel 7 is indeed the divine Messiah of Christian theology. When Jesus described Himself by the title "Son of Man" more than any other title, He was not only identifying Himself as the subject of this

SON OF MAN TAKES DOMINION

magnificent prophecy, but also identifying Himself as the fulfillment of all the prophecies that came before it. Jesus knew exactly who He was—and He wanted everyone else to know.

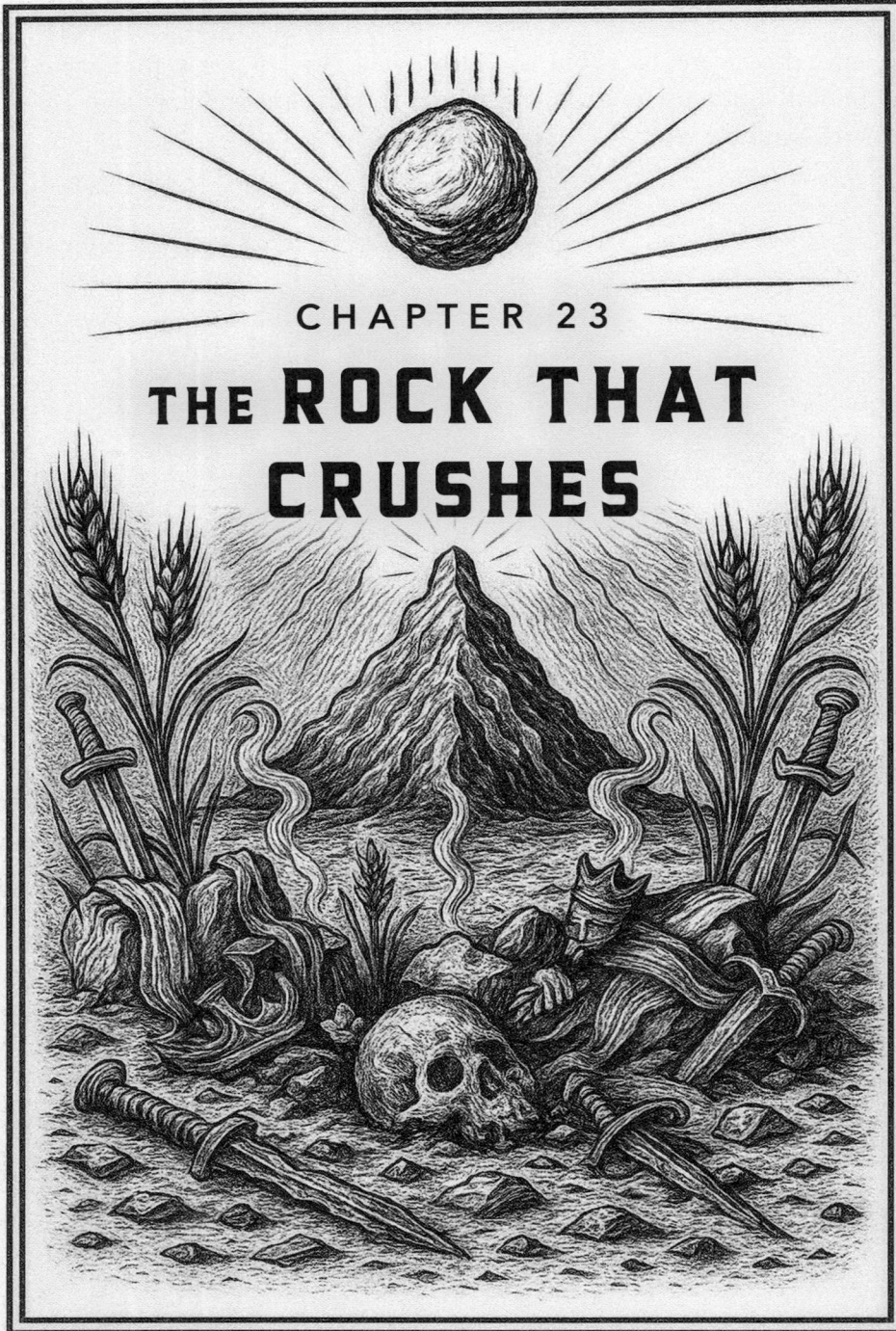

CHAPTER 23

THE ROCK THAT CRUSHES

THROUGHOUT HISTORY, the two seed lines have continued to clash. One seed-line will culminate with a King who will crush evil, redeem creation, and restore all that has been lost. The other seed-line—the seed-line of the serpent—saw various pagan rulers and their kingdoms serve as precursors, prophetic pre-echos of the ultimate final beast. In the prophecy of Daniel, the details concerning the destruction of this final serpent kingdom come into clear focus.

In Daniel chapter 2, we read about a dream given to the pagan king Nebuchadnezzar. It was a very troubling dream—a colossal statue made of various precious and strong metals. Though it dazzled with its imposing glory, its meaning was ominous. None of the king's advisors could interpret it. But God revealed the meaning to His servant Daniel.

> "You saw, O king, and behold, a great image. This image, mighty and of exceeding brightness, stood before you, and its appearance was frightening. The head of this image was of fine gold, its chest and arms of silver, its middle and thighs of bronze, its legs of iron, its feet partly of iron and partly of clay." (Daniel 2:31–33)

Daniel explained that each segment of the statue represented a different kingdom: The head of gold represents Babylon, the chest and arms of silver represent Medo-Persia, the belly and thighs of bronze represent Greece, and then there is one final kingdom made of iron. The feet of the statue would be a mixture of hard iron and brittle clay. But the real climax of the dream wasn't the statue at all. It is what happened next.

> "You continued looking until a stone was cut out without hands, and it struck the statue on its feet of iron and clay and crushed them. Then the iron, the clay, the bronze, the silver and the gold were crushed all at the same time and became like chaff from the summer threshing floors; and the wind carried them away so that not a trace of them was found. But the stone that struck the statue became a great mountain and filled the whole earth." (Daniel 2:34–35)

This stone, or rock, cut without human hands, represents the coming Messianic Kingdom. It is not crafted by human strength or political genius. It does not rise through elections or armies. Rather, it comes from heaven. It strikes with utter devastation and finality. After it strikes, all of the proud kingdoms of man crumble to dust and disappear.

In this prophecy, the Rock is the Promised One—the Messiah. It represents both the return of the King and the establishment of His Kingdom here on the earth.

THE TIMING OF THE STRIKE

What is most crucial to understand is the ferocity of the strike and its timing. The kingdom of God is not described as quietly arriving and slowly transforming the world from within. The passage describes a sudden, dramatic, and definitive shattering of the statue. Daniel's description leaves no room for ambiguity. The statue is not dismantled bit by bit or piece by piece. It is shattered, completely pulverized, in an instant. It is then swept away like chaff in the wind. In the end, only the Messianic Kingdom remains:

> "Then the iron, the clay, the bronze, the silver, and the gold, all together were broken in pieces, and became like the chaff of the summer threshing floors; and the wind carried them away... and the stone... became a great mountain and filled the whole earth." (Daniel 2:35)

Again, this is no slow, gradual process. Instead, Daniel describes a swift and definitive judgment. This is the Day of the Lord—the moment when Jesus returns to crush His enemies under His feet. It is the climax of redemptive history.

GIVEN TO THE SAINTS

The pattern frequently seen through the Bible is that the suffering of God's people precedes their deliverance. Even the Skull Crusher would

NEBUCHADNEZZAR'S DREAM OF A TOWERING STATUE

suffer before reigning. Before being exalted, the Servant would Himself be pierced and crushed. So too, in the prophecy of Daniel, the same pattern is repeated. In Daniel 7, before this never-ending kingdom is given to the saints, first they will suffer at the hand of this final beast. A wicked ruler will arise and wage war against them, and for a short time, it will seem as though he has won:

> "I kept looking, and that horn was waging war with the saints and over-powering them until the Ancient of Days came, and judgment was passed in favor of the saints of the Highest One, and the time arrived when the saints took possession of the kingdom." (Daniel 7:21–22)

The Rock does not strike during peace and prosperity. It strikes in the midst of tremendous suffering. It strikes when the saints are being crushed. When the Rock comes, however, everything changes.

As we discussed in the previous chapter, when the King returns, He will restore the throne of David, and the kingdom will be given to the saints. Persecution and suffering will come to a sudden and immediate end.

THE EMPIRE THAT WAS NEVER BROKEN

Some argue that the coming of the Rock represents Jesus' first coming, and the subsequent slow and gradual decline of the Roman Empire that followed fulfills the prophecy. This view, however, does not align with what the passage says. Think about this: Was the Roman Empire wholly and suddenly shattered in the first century? Did it become as chaff and disappear? Quite to the contrary. The Roman Empire continued to grow and persecute Christians for hundreds of years, long after Jesus. Even after Constantine, who in the fourth century adopted Christianity as the official state religion, the Roman Empire continued to exist for centuries, eventually evolving into the Byzantine Empire. It was not until 1453 that the eastern wing of the empire finally fell to Mehmet Fatih and his Ottoman armies.

So, Jesus came, but the kingdoms of man were not swept away as the vision describes. The statue still stands. We continue to await the Rock to come and strike the brittle feet. When Jesus returns, He will come not only as the Skull Crusher, but as the Kingdom-Crusher.

KINGDOMS IN COLLISION

The dream given to Nebuchadnezzar is not merely ancient history. It is prophecy. It refers to the climax of the biblical story, when the rule of man comes to an end. The Rock is indeed still coming.

When it strikes, there will be no election, no recount. There will be no loopholes. The kingdoms of this world will become as dust as they all become the kingdom of our Lord and His Messiah, and He will reign forever and ever (Revelation 11:15).

> "And in the days of those kings, the God of heaven will set up a kingdom that shall never be destroyed... It shall break in pieces all these kingdoms and bring them to an end, and it shall stand forever." (Daniel 2:44)

OUR UNSHAKABLE HOPE

The message of the Bible is clear: Judgment is coming. And for many, that might feel ominous. But for the people of God, it is the most hopeful news in the world. Because when the Rock strikes, persecution and oppression will cease. The mockers and oppressors will be silenced. The saints will inherit the everlasting kingdom. Until then, we eagerly await the Seed of the Woman, the Skull Crusher, the Seed of Abraham, the Lion of Judah, the Greater Moses, the Cloud Rider, the Desert Marcher, the Suffering Servant, the Coming King—the Rock that Crushes. Take heart.

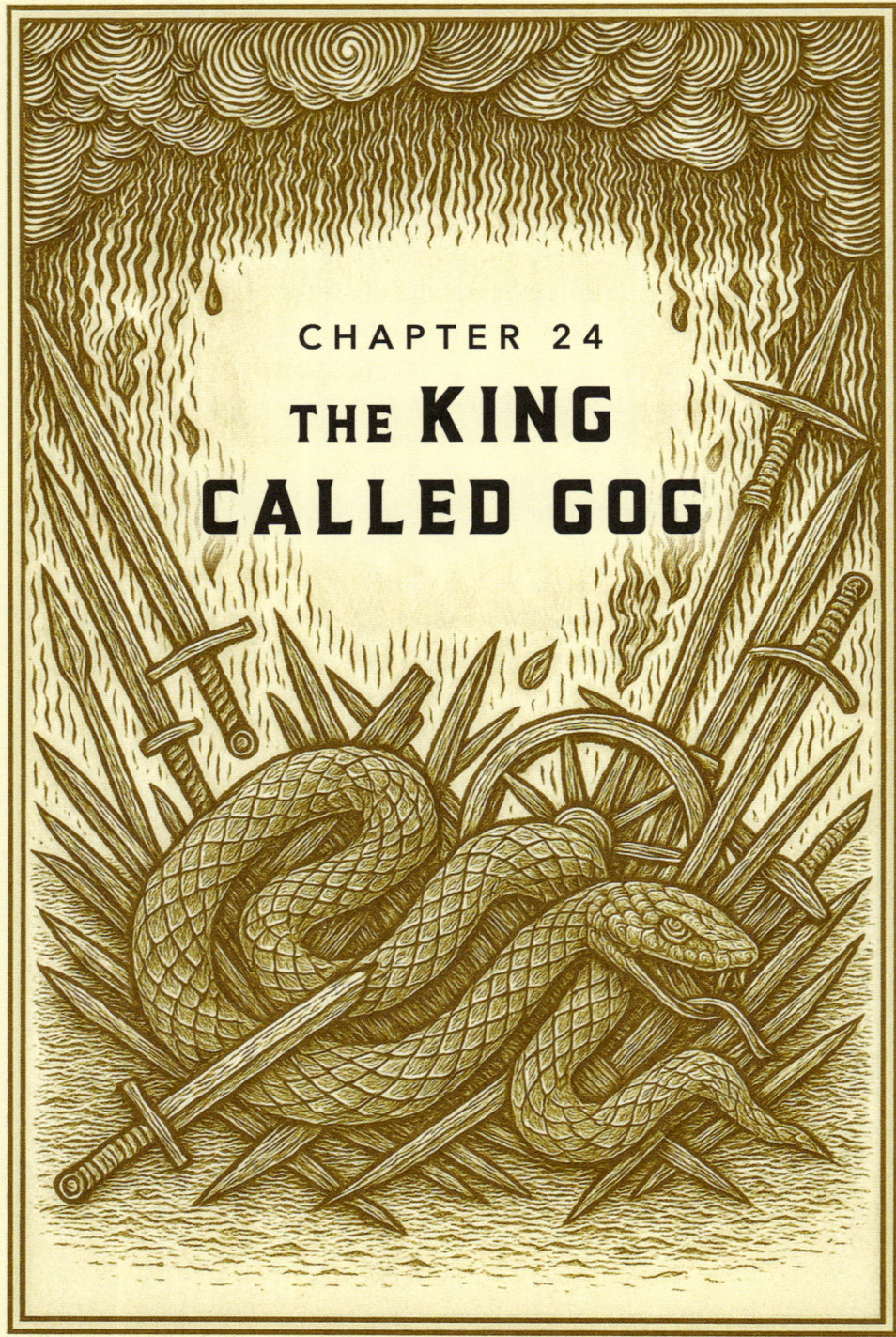

CHAPTER 24

THE KING CALLED GOG

FROM GENESIS TO REVELATION, the Scriptures sketch a single, continuous storyline of war—a cosmic conflict between the seed of the woman and the seed of the serpent (Gen. 3:15). This ancient feud finds expression in countless historical narratives, each episode functioning as a signpost pointing toward the ultimate showdown between the Messiah and His archenemy, the Antichrist. Pharaoh, Sisera, Goliath—all prefigure the final Beast. Nowhere is this thread more vividly portrayed than in the prophetic visions of Daniel and Ezekiel, culminating in the apocalyptic figures known as "the little horn" or "Gog."

GOG: THE FINAL EMBODIMENT OF THE SERPENT'S SEED

Ezekiel 38–39 describes a vast military coalition led by "Gog, of the land of Magog," who gathers a multitude of nations to assault Israel in the last days. For many interpreters, Gog is a mysterious figure isolated to these chapters. But God Himself, in Ezekiel 38:17, insists otherwise: "Are you not the one I spoke of in former times by my servants the prophets of Israel?" He asks. The Septuagint directly states: "You are the one." This declaration reveals that Gog is not new to the prophetic story—he is the culmination of a line of enemy-kings foreshadowed throughout the Old Testament.

Indeed, the Septuagint version of Balaam's prophecy in Numbers 24 reads, "His king shall be greater than Gog" (v. 7). Unlike most modern translations, it is not Agag, but Gog. This same variant is found in other, more ancient readings of the passages. These include the Samaritan Pentateuch and three different early Jewish translations. This ancient reading reveals that Balaam foresaw a future king from Israel who would crush Gog, the final eschatological enemy of God's people. Gog is the name Balaam uses for the final Beast—the last and greatest seed of the serpent. Balaam's prophecy was not just about David's temporary victory over Moab or Saul's victory over the Amalekites, but a forecast of the Messiah's ultimate triumph over the Antichrist.

GOG THE KING

DANIEL'S LITTLE HORN AND KING OF THE NORTH:
THE FINAL ADVERSARY

In both Daniel 7 and 8, the final adversary appears as a "little horn"—a cunning, blasphemous, and genocidal figure who wages war against the saints. Though Antiochus IV Epiphanes partially fulfilled these prophecies, Gabriel the Archangel explicitly tells Daniel that the ultimate fulfillment of the vision will take place "at the time of the end" (Dan. 8:17, 19). Antiochus, like Pharaoh and the other snake-kings, serves as a prototype of a greater tyrant yet to come.

Daniel 11 also reinforces this storyline. There, in verses 21–35 we find a detailed description of the historical Antiochus, but in verse 36 the focus shifts to a new, future king who "exalts himself above every god" and is ultimately destroyed by divine intervention (Dan. 11:45). There he is called "the King of the North," a title used repeatedly throughout the chapter to describe Seleucid rulers from the Syrian region—pointing to a Middle Eastern origin for the final Antichrist.

Critically, the Antichrist and Gog share identical characteristics: both invade Israel when she feels secure (Dan. 8:25; 11:24; Ezek. 38:11), both are destroyed by divine judgment (Dan. 8:25; Ezek. 39:4), and both fall in the land of Israel, where their corpses become food for birds (Ezek. 39:17–20; Rev. 19:17–18). These are not two separate eschatological enemies—they are one and the same.

PHARAOH, SISERA, AND GOLIATH: THE PATTERN REPEATED

Just as Gog synthesizes the language and actions of previous tyrants, so too does he recapitulate their role in the larger biblical story. Pharaoh's proud defiance of YHVH, Sisera's deceptive peace before judgment, and Goliath's blasphemous arrogance all prefigure Gog's final rebellion. Each of these enemies met their end through a surprising twist of divine justice—drowned, pierced, or crushed.

In Exodus, Pharaoh hardens his heart and is ultimately overthrown by YHVH in a dramatic, public demonstration of power. Similarly, Gog's demise at the hands of the Messiah will be sudden, supernatural,

THE SEEDS OF THE SERPENT

and universally witnessed (Ezek. 39:6–8).

Judges 4 depicts a foreign general named Sisera, who was destroyed by the hand of an unexpected woman, her hammer and her tent peg. Ezekiel 38 likewise emphasizes Israel's apparent false sense of peace before Gog's invasion, exposing his reliance on deceit and surprise—hallmarks of the Antichrist's campaign (Dan. 11:24).

Goliath, the Philistine champion, through his arrogance, towering presence, and open defiance of Israel's God, mirrors the Antichrist's last days blasphemies. Both are defeated not through military power, but through divinely empowered agents—David in the case of Goliath, and the Messiah Himself in the case of Gog.

Each of these stories is more than a little historical vignette—they are typologies, shadows cast by the same ancient adversary: the serpent. In both the prophecy of Balaam and in Ezekiel's prophecy, Gog is the final seed of the serpent.

THE FINAL WAR: DANIEL AND EZEKIEL IN HARMONY

Altogether, the portrait painted by Daniel 8, 11, and Ezekiel 38–39 presents a coherent and sobering picture of the end-time war. The Antichrist will arise from the north (Dan. 11:40; Ezek. 38:15), conquer multiple nations (Dan. 11:42–43), and deceive Israel with a false peace (Dan. 9:27; Ezek. 38:11). His reign will culminate in a final invasion of the land of Israel, where he will meet his doom at the hands of the returning King—the Holy One of Israel, visibly present in the land (Ezek. 39:7, 21–22).

This is not a minor or optional doctrinal detail. This vision completes the prophetic expectation of the Day of the Lord. The nations rage, all the vipers gather together in alliance, but the Son of David rides forth in glory to strike down the beast and crush the serpent's head—once and for all.

THE PATTERN AND THE PROMISE

What began as a whispered promise in Eden has become the defining storyline of Scripture. The seed of the woman will crush the serpent. Pharaoh, Sisera, Goliath, and Antiochus—all were shadows cast by the coming final Beast, who himself will be slain by the brilliance of the Coming One. For those with eyes to see, Scriptures are clear: Daniel's Little Horn, the King of the North, Ezekiel's Gog, are not separate individuals, but multiple revelations of a singular, climactic enemy of God and His people—the final Beast. Thus, the prophecy of Ezekiel 38-39, upon describing the destruction of Gog and his hordes, proceeds to describe the culmination of redemptive history, the salvation and the restoration of the Kingdom of Israel:

> Therefore thus says the Lord God, "Now I will restore the fortunes of Jacob and have mercy on the whole house of Israel; and I will be jealous for My holy name. They will forget their disgrace and all their treachery which they perpetrated against Me, when they live securely on their own land with no one to make them afraid. When I bring them back from the peoples and gather them from the lands of their enemies, then I shall be sanctified through them in the sight of the many nations. Then they will know that I am the Lord their God because I made them go into exile among the nations, and then gathered them again to their own land; and I will leave none of them there any longer. I will not hide My face from them any longer, for I will have poured out My Spirit on the house of Israel," declares the Lord God. (Ezekiel 39:25–29).

Not only is all of Israel restored and living safely back in their own land, but they also have come to know God, and He has poured out His Spirit on them, speaking of the glorious day when all Israel will be saved.

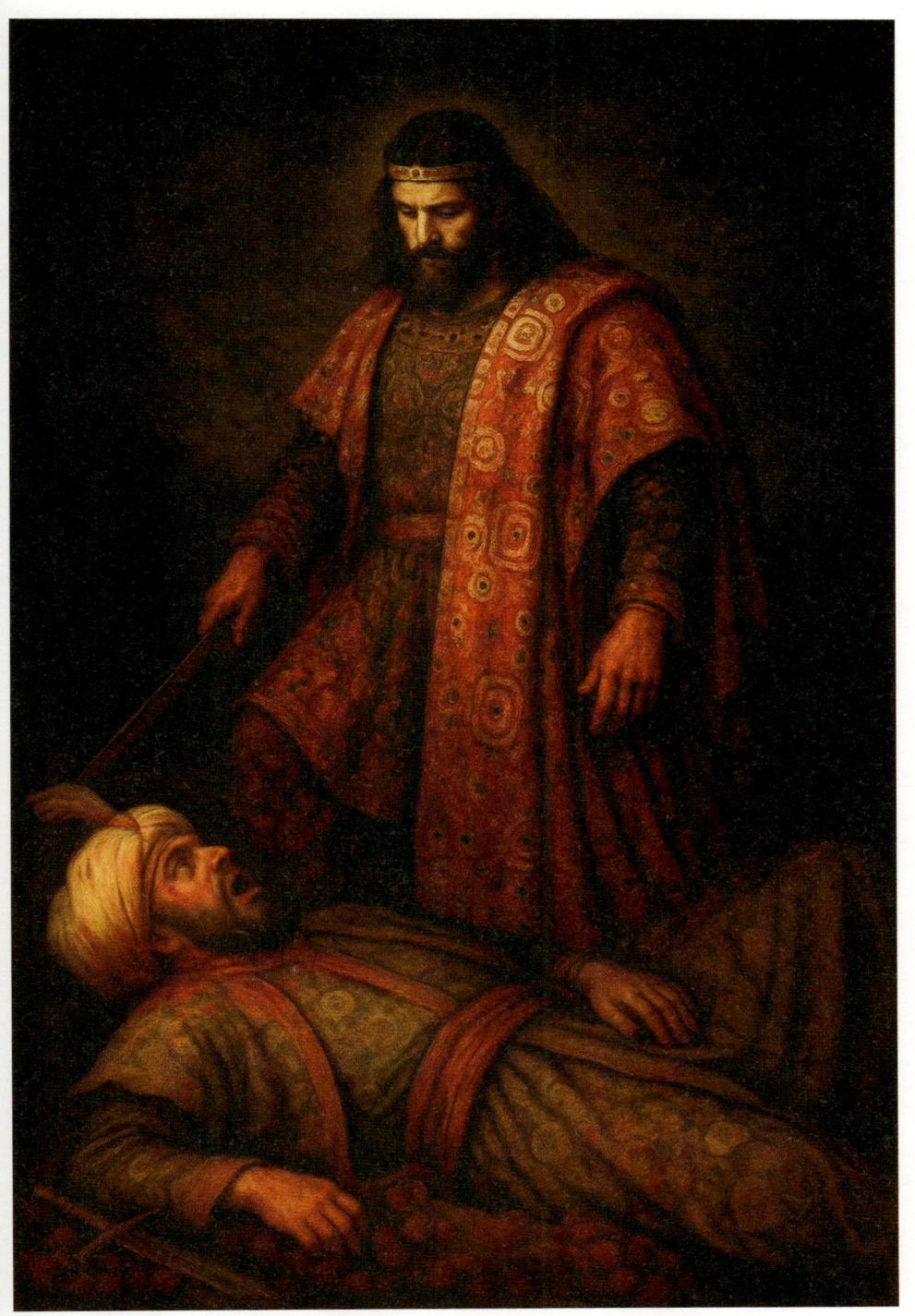

DEATH OF GOG

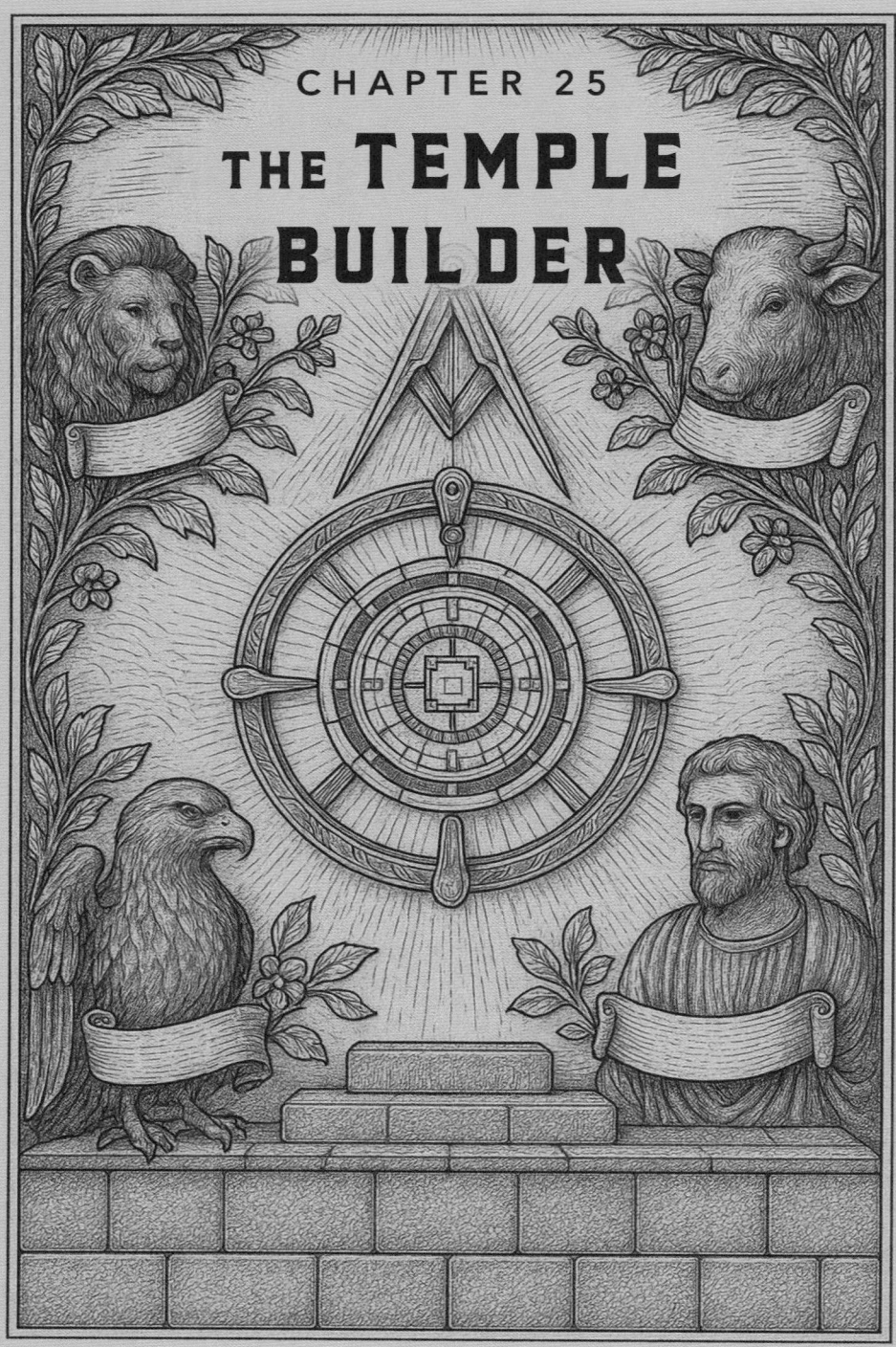

CHAPTER 25

THE TEMPLE BUILDER

FROM THE BEGINNING OF THE BIBLICAL STORY to its climactic end, one thread remains constant: God desires to dwell with His people. Eden was the first sanctuary. There, God walked with humanity in perfect fellowship. After sin shattered that intimacy, the Lord continually reestablished His presence at Sinai, in the Tabernacle, and in the temple at Jerusalem. Yet each of these sanctuaries was either defiled or destroyed. Still, the plan never changed. God has always intended to make His home among us—fully, permanently, and gloriously.

As the prophets looked forward to the coming of the Messiah, they saw not only a King, a Priest, a Redeemer, and a Judge—they also saw a Builder. A Temple Builder. The One who would restore the dwelling place of God on earth.

A ROYAL SON WHO BUILDS

The promise of a coming temple builder was first given in God's covenant with David. When David offered to build a house for the Lord, the Lord responded by turning the tables—David would not build for God; instead, God would build a dynasty for David:

> "When your days are finished and you lie down with your fathers, I
> will raise up your descendant after you, who will come from you, and
> I will establish his kingdom. He shall build a house for My name, and
> I will establish the throne of his kingdom forever" (2 Samuel 7:12–13).

At first, this prophecy appears to point to Solomon, who indeed built the first temple in Jerusalem. Yet the promise extends beyond Solomon. This royal son would have an eternal throne. He would be uniquely God's son (v. 14). And unlike Solomon's divided and eventually fallen kingdom, this future King's reign would never end.

Thus, the Davidic covenant is also a messianic prophecy. The Messiah—the ultimate Son of David—will reign forever. But more than that, He will build the house of the Lord.

THE TEMPLE BUILDER

THE PRIEST-KING OF ZECHARIAH

This expectation is sharpened centuries later through the prophet Zechariah. In a symbolic act, Zechariah is commanded to crown the high priest Joshua (Yehoshua—"the Lord saves") and declare:

> "Behold, there is a man whose name is Branch, for He will branch out from where He is; and He will build the temple of the Lord. Yes, it is He who will build the temple of the Lord, and He who will bear the honor and sit and rule on His throne. So He will be a priest on His throne, and the counsel of peace will be between the two offices" (Zechariah 6:12–13).

This "Branch" is the same royal figure foretold in Isaiah 11:1 and Jeremiah 23:5—a descendant of David who would reign in righteousness. But now he is revealed as both King and Priest. He will unite both offices in Himself and build the true temple of God.

This remarkable figure can be none other than the Messiah—Jesus, the Son of David, and our Great High Priest. Having offered Himself as the final sacrifice, He now intercedes for us from the heavenly sanctuary. But His priestly work will not always remain spiritual, invisible, in heaven. He will return to establish visible justice, restore worship on earth, and build the physical temple of the Lord in Jerusalem.

EZEKIEL'S TEMPLE VISION AND DANIEL'S TIMETABLE

Nowhere is this hope described more fully than in the closing chapters of Ezekiel. There, the prophet is taken to a high mountain in the land of Israel, where he sees an immense and holy temple complex, unlike anything that had ever existed. Its measurements are exact. It is a written blueprint. From its threshold flows a river of life that brings healing to the nations (Ezek. 47).

The vision also introduces a mysterious figure known simply as "the Prince" (Ezek. 44–46). He leads worship, offers sacrifices, and presides over feast days. Some view him as a resurrected David or a subordinate ruler under the Messiah. Others propose he is a human prince ruling during the Messianic Age. The prince also has sons and participates in sin offerings; thus, it is best to see him as a Davidic ruler, a messianic deputy in a restored kingdom, but not Jesus Himself.

Still, the temple itself—and the broader context of Ezekiel's vision—points unmistakably toward the future. The second temple never matched Ezekiel's specifications, nor will the coming third temple. The vision awaits fulfillment in the messianic age.

Strikingly, Daniel's prophetic visions offer corroborating details. In Daniel 8:13–14, an angelic figure speaks of 2,300 evenings and mornings—a period that will not pass until "the sanctuary is properly restored." This implies a literal sanctuary that has been defiled and will be rededicated.

The harmony between Ezekiel's temple vision and Daniel's prophetic calendar paints a consistent picture: the end of the age will culminate not only in judgment and resurrection but also in the physical restoration of the house of the Lord, filled with His glory.

A TEMPLE GREATER THAN SOLOMON'S

When Jesus walked through the temple courts during His earthly ministry, He made a staggering claim:

> "Destroy this temple, and in three days I will raise it up" (John 2:19).

Those listening misunderstood, assuming He meant the physical structure. But John explains: "He was speaking about the temple of His body" (v. 21).

In Jesus, the promise began to be fulfilled in an unexpected way. He is Immanuel—God with us. The divine presence dwells bodily in Him (Col. 2:9). But this was only the beginning. After His resurrection, He ascended into heaven, and He will return—not only to raise the dead, judge the nations, and reign from Zion, but also to rebuild the sanctuary of the Lord. His redemptive work will come full circle in the restoration of Eden.

EZEKIEL'S VISION OF MESSIAH'S TEMPLE

The apostles never taught that the temple promises were canceled or spiritualized away. Instead, Peter declared that Jesus must remain in heaven "until the period of restoration of all things" (Acts 3:21). This includes the throne of David, the kingdom of Israel, and the house of the Lord.

THE DWELLING PLACE OF GOD

The final vision in Scripture reveals the consummation of all that the temple foreshadowed. John sees the New Jerusalem descending from heaven, and he hears a loud voice:

> "Behold, the tabernacle of God is among the people, and He will dwell among them, and they shall be His people" (Revelation 21:3).

Then comes this astounding declaration:

> "I saw no temple in it, for the Lord God the Almighty and the Lamb are its temple" (v. 22).

This is not a negation of the temple—it is the final fulfillment. Every temple, from Eden to Ezekiel's vision, was a shadow pointing forward to this: the unmediated presence of God with His people, forever.

This eternal city, however, comes after the thousand-year reign of Christ (Rev. 20:16). Throughout the millennium, the nations will come to Zion, the law will go forth from Jerusalem, and the house of the Lord will be a house of prayer for all peoples (Isa. 2:2–4; Zech. 14:16). The temple in the Millennium will be a real, physical sanctuary where redeemed humanity will participate in the worship that takes place there.

THE BUILDER IS COMING

The Messiah is not only the King and Priest—He is the Builder of God's house. Greater than Solomon, He will restore what sin ruined. He will cleanse the sanctuary, rededicate the altar, and fill the house with glory.

He is the Branch, the Cornerstone, the Son of David and Son of God. In Him, the priesthood and kingship are united. Through Him, God's eternal dwelling with man will be established. We await not only a Ruler and Redeemer, but the One who will fulfill every promise concerning the house of the Lord.

"He will build His house, and the glory of the latter house will be greater than the former" (Haggai 2:9).

THE CORNERSTONE THE BUILDERS REJECTED

CHAPTER 26

THE PIERCED ONE

THE PROPHET ZECHARIAH STANDS at a critical juncture in redemptive history. As one of the post-exilic prophets, he lived after the return from the Babylonian captivity. The temple was being rebuilt, but was not nearly complete. Into this fragile moment, Zechariah speaks with a voice that echoes all the prophets who came before—and with a clarity that pierces the fog.

Drawing from the entire tapestry of messianic expectation—Genesis, Exodus, Psalms, Isaiah, Daniel, and Zechariah — gives us some of the most vivid, apocalyptic, and theologically rich visions in the entire Bible. His words leap across centuries, pointing both to the suffering of the Messiah and the showdown in Jerusalem before the Messiah's return.

More than any other prophet, Zechariah gives us a window into both the suffering and the triumph of the Messiah—a vision of the Pierced One who returns in glory to save His people and assume the throne.

THE LORD MARCHES IN THE WHIRLWIND

Like Enoch, Moses, Hannah, Habakkuk, Isaiah, and David before him, Zechariah sees the Lord coming in power from the south:

> "Then the Lord will appear over them, And His arrow will go forth like lightning; And the Lord God will blow the trumpet, And march in the storm winds of the south." (Zechariah 9:14)

This is the language of divine war. "The storm winds of the south" recall Deuteronomy 33, Psalm 68, Habakkuk 3, and Isaiah 63—all passages where the God of Sinai is portrayed as a Warrior-King marching toward Jerusalem. Zechariah reintroduces this same vision: YHVH, the Divine Warrior, will appear in the skies to save His people at their darkest hour. The return of the King will be no quiet affair—it will be a cosmic military confrontation.

THE ONE THEY PIERCED

At the heart of Zechariah's prophetic vision of God appearing in the sky is a moment of heartbreak and revelation:

> "They will look on Me whom they have pierced, And they will mourn for Him, As one mourns for an only son." (Zechariah 12:10)

This verse is staggering. The speaker is YHVH—"they will look on Me"—and yet He refers to mourning "for Him," the One who was pierced. God is identifying Himself with the suffering of the Messiah.

Zechariah is drawing from Psalm 22, where the righteous one is pierced. But he presses further. The mourning is corporate, national. The people of Israel will recognize the One they once rejected, and their hearts will be broken. Yet this heartbreak will not lead to despair. Instead, it will unlock a river of mercy:

> "In that day a fountain will be opened For the house of David and for the inhabitants of Jerusalem, For sin and for impurity." (Zechariah 13:1)

The pierced wound becomes the wellspring of cleansing. This is the gospel: the crucified King opens a fountain of mercy that washes away sin.

THE FINAL SIEGE AND THE CRY FOR DELIVERANCE

Before this glorious return, however, comes darkness. Zechariah describes a final, devastating siege of Jerusalem:

> "Behold, a day is coming for the Lord... I will gather all the nations against Jerusalem to battle, And the city will be captured, The houses plundered, the women raped, And half of the city exiled..." (Zechariah 14:1–2)

THE ONE THEY HAVE PIERCED

This is not poetic hyperbole. It is a prophecy of brutal reality. The holy city will again be invaded, and the people will suffer greatly. But as we've seen, this will not be the end. "Then the Lord will go forth and fight against those nations..." (v. 3). This moment of divine intervention parallels Daniel 7, where the final beast wages war against the saints and appears to prevail:

> "That horn was waging war with the saints and overpowering them, until the Ancient of Days came and judgment was passed in favor of the saints of the Highest One." (Daniel 7:21–22)

Just when all seems lost, the pierced One will return—not in humility, but in fury.

THE KING DESCENDS

Zechariah continues:

> "On that day His feet will stand on the Mount of Olives... And the Mount will be split in its middle from east to west." (Zechariah 14:4)

The very earth trembles at His arrival. This is no vague spiritual return. The same King who ascended will descend—visibly, bodily, gloriously. And He will not come alone:

> "Then the Lord my God will come, And all the holy ones with Him!" (Zechariah 14:5)

This is the fulfillment of Jude 14–15, where Enoch prophesied, "Behold, the Lord comes with ten thousands of His holy ones." It is the day foreseen in Psalm 2 and Revelation 19. Heaven will open, and the armies of the Lamb will descend.

THE PROPHET OF CONVERGENCE

Zechariah is the prophet of convergence. His visions bring together the themes of Genesis, the Psalms, Isaiah, Daniel, and the Torah. In his words, we see the Messiah as: The Shepherd who is struck (Zech. 13:7), the One who is pierced (Zech. 12:10), the Divine Warrior who marches in the storm (Zech. 9:14) and the One whose return will split the Mount of Olives (Zech. 14:4).

Zechariah gives us a Messiah who suffers, but who will return. The One we pierced is not dead. He is alive. And when He returns, the siege will be broken. The fountain of forgiveness and mercy will flow. The Kingdom will be restored.

HE WILL MARCH IN THE WHIRLWINDS OF THE SOUTH

CHAPTER 27

THE SUN OF RIGHTEOUSNESS

FROM THE EARLIEST PAGES OF SCRIPTURE, God is associated with radiant glory, not just as a metaphor for His holiness, but as a kind of actual physical reality. Paul the Apostle tells us generally that God "alone possesses immortality and dwells in unapproachable light, whom no one has seen or can see." (1 Tim 6:16). The theme of God shining like the sun, however, is most emphasized through the Scriptures when it describes His return or His coming from heaven.

The first appearance of this imagery is found in Deuteronomy 33, where Moses blesses the tribes of Israel just before his death. There, it is said that He "dawned on them from Seir; He shone forth from Mount Paran" (Dt 33:2). YHVH is described as marching from the wilderness in radiant, sun-like brilliance. Shining over the tall mountains to the south of Israel, it is not the rays of the morning sun, as the sun rises in the east—this is the Lord God Himself. His coming is consistently described as being like the dawn. His glory is like the rising sun. Again, this is not just a metaphor—it is the nature of God's real presence.

This pattern continues in both the Psalms and the Prophets.

THE SPLENDOR OF THE MORNING STAR

In Habakkuk, the glory of the coming One is unmistakably solar. Like Moses before him, Habakkuk describes the Lord, whose "splendor covers the heavens," whose "radiance is like the sunlight," and who has rays of light beaming forth, "flashing from His hand" (Hab 3:3–4). God is again coming from the south, from the desert, glowing with radiant glory.

Isaiah also joins the chorus. The expectant saints are told to "Arise, shine; for your light has come, and the glory of the Lord has risen upon you" (Is 60:1). Isaiah then reminds us that it is always darkest just before the breaking forth of the dawn:

"For behold, darkness will cover the earth
and deep darkness the peoples,
but the Lord will rise upon you
and His glory will appear upon you." (Isaiah 60:1–2)

THE SUN OF RIGHTEOUSNESS

Once again, YHVH is described as rising, not poetically, but as a very real physical description. As one can feel the warmth of the sun on their skin, so also will the day come when the righteous will feel the comforting glow of the Lord's glory on their skin. This is the hope not only of the remnant of Israel but of all nations:

> "Nations will come to your light, And kings to the brightness of your rising." (Isaiah 60:3)

As a result of seeing such heavenly glory, like Moses—whose face would shine after speaking to God face to face—so also will the righteous observers themselves shine on that day:

> "Then you will see and be radiant, And your heart will thrill and rejoice;" (v. 5)

THE FINAL DAWN IN MALACHI

The climax of this imagery is found in the final prophetic voice of the Old Testament. First, we are given one of the most precious descriptions in the Bible. On that day, we will be like a young calf, who leaps from its pen, skipping about with joy, in the spring grass:

> "But for you who fear My name, the sun of righteousness will rise with healing in its wings; and you will go forth and skip about like calves from the stall." (Malachi 4:2)

Then the passage quickly takes a darker turn, returning to the theme of God's enemies being crushed underfoot:

> "You will tread down the wicked, for they will be ashes under the soles of your feet on the day which I am preparing," (v. 3).

SKIPPING LIKE CALVES FROM THEIR STALLS

YOU WILL TREAD UPON THE ASHES OF THE WICKED

YHVH is not merely likened to the sun—He is called the Sun of Righteousness. His arrival will bring both healing and judgment. For the righteous, His wings (a Hebrew idiom referring to the rays of the sun) bring renewal and restoration. For the wicked, His rising brings devastation and judgment. The faithful will not only rejoice; they will dance, skip, and tread upon the ashes of the enemies of God.

Again, this is not merely a poetic flourish. It is the justice that has been promised ever since Eden. It is the fulfillment of Genesis 3:15. The seed of the woman crushes the head of the serpent. The children of the seed walk victorious. The wicked are as dust beneath their feet. This is not a cocky triumphalism. It is the final vindication of the righteous and the oppressed of the earth. This is why Paul the Apostle would later declare that "The God of peace will soon crush Satan under your feet" (Rom 16:20).

LIGHTNING OR LIGHTING?

Our journey through the Old Testament, examining the various messianic prophecies and the storyline of the Skull Crusher, has reached its end. The transition into the New Testament begins. Having looked at a few of the most important passages that portray the return of the Lord, and how He will come in radiant shining light, this is an opportune moment to bring clarity to one of the difficult sayings of Jesus. In Matthew 24:27, Jesus is recorded saying: "For just as the lightning comes from the east and flashes even to the west, so will the coming of the Son of Man be." The Greek term used here for lightning (*astrapē*) is ambiguous. It can mean "lightning" as in a lightning bolt, but it can also mean the shining radiance of the morning light. Because Jesus specifically says that this "lightning" will flash from "east to west," we see that He was alluding to these prophecies: Deuteronomy 33, Habakkuk 3, Isaiah 60, and Micah 4. Jesus was not saying His return will be like an electrical storm or lightning bolt, which bursts forth in nearly any direction it chooses. He is saying that His coming will be like the dawn—inescapable, visible to all, sudden and glorious. He will

LIKE LIGHTENING FROM THE EAST TO WEST

rise over the world as the Sun of Righteousness, just as the prophets foresaw. This is why Peter later calls Him "the Morning Star" (2 Peter 1:19), and Revelation calls Him "the Bright Morning Star" (Revelation 22:16). Jesus is the light of the world. He is "the sunrise from on high" (Luke 1:78). And when He comes, the long night will finally end.

Maranatha!

Arise, O Sun of Righteousness.

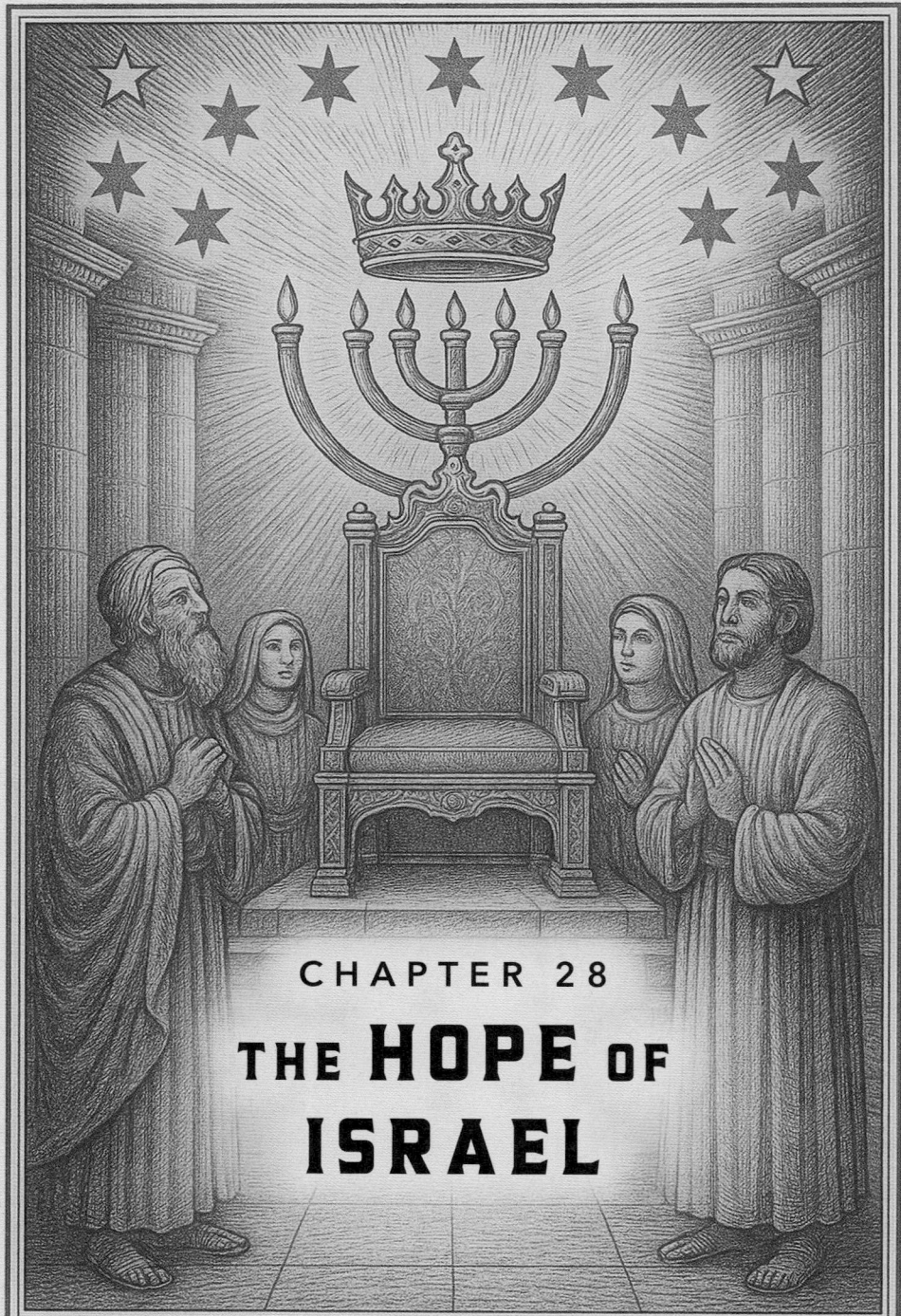

CHAPTER 28

THE **HOPE** OF **ISRAEL**

BY THE CLOSE OF THE OLD TESTAMENT PERIOD, the Jewish people had a vibrant and well-developed belief in a coming King-Messiah who would restore the Kingdom of Israel and rule the entire earth. These expectations were consistently upheld by devout and biblically informed Jews during Jesus' time. More importantly, Jesus Himself affirmed and taught all of these exact expectations. The entire New Testament continues to uphold and champion all of the promises God made to Israel—clearly, literally, and consistently.

THE GENEALOGIES OF JESUS

In the very first verse of the New Testament, the hope of Israel is reiterated. Matthew 1:1 very purposely highlights Jesus' physical lineage:

> "The record of the genealogy of Jesus the Messiah, the son of David, the son of Abraham."

Why is this so important? Because, according to the Scriptures, the Messiah must be a literal descendant, the "seed" of both Abraham and King David. Thus, Matthew immediately identifies Jesus as the fulfillment of the covenant promises made to both men. Jesus is presented as the promised seed of Eve, Abraham, and David—the One all the prophets had anticipated! Similarly, Mark's Gospel begins,

> "The beginning of the gospel of Jesus Christ, the Son of God" (Mark 1:1).

By referring to Jesus as the "Son of God," Mark alludes to the Davidic Covenant and Messianic prophecies like Psalm 2: "You are My Son, today I have begotten You."

Both Matthew and Mark root their gospel introductions in the covenants and prophecies of the Old Testament. The first verses in the first two gospels both appeal directly back to the Davidic Covenant. The first verse in the New Testament anticipates the literal fulfillment of God's promises.

THE TESTIMONY OF GABRIEL TO MARY

In Luke's Gospel, the pattern continues. The angel Gabriel's announcement to Mary is mind-blowing in so many ways. It begins:

"The angel Gabriel was sent from God to a city in Galilee called Nazareth, to a virgin engaged to a man whose name was Joseph, of the descendants of David; and the virgin's name was Mary" (vv. 26-27).

Gabriel declared to her:

"Do not be afraid, Mary; for you have found favor with God. And behold, you will conceive in your womb and bear a son, and you shall name Him Jesus." (v. 31).

Jesus (*Yeshua* in Hebrew) means, "YHVH Saves." But it is the next portion of the announcement that is so stunning. Gabriel then said:

"He will be great and will be called the Son of the Most High; and the Lord God will give Him the throne of His father David; and He will reign over the house of Jacob forever, and His kingdom will have no end" (v. 32).

Gabriel's statement is filled with such clear Old Testament allusions! Imagine how this would have been understood by Mary, a faithful Jew, so thoroughly acquainted with the Old Testament. Her son would be the One to rule on the throne of His father David, whose kingdom would have no end. Her mind would have jumped back to the Davidic Covenant and other prophecies such as Isaiah 9. Her son would be the "child born to us" who would reestablish the throne of His father David on Mount Zion; He is the One who would restore the Kingdom of Israel! He would be the One who would be called, "Wonderful Counselor, Mighty God, Eternal Father, Prince of Peace" (Is 9:6). Imagine Mary's heart racing as she realized that it was her son whose

THE ANNUNCIATION

kingdom would have no end. His rule would bring a great blessing to all the nations of the world. Imagine the shock she felt when she made the connection to so many other glorious prophecies. Was her child truly to be the One who would someday come from heaven in blazing fire with myriads of angels to judge the wicked? (1En 1:9; Ps 110:1, 5-6; Is 25:10; 34; 63:6) Was He to be the One who would undo the curse of the fall, and give His people rest? (Gen 5:28–29) Could it be true that her son was the One who would someday crush the head of Satan and his followers? (Gen 3:15; Num 24:17-20) Indeed, being familiar with the Hebrew Scriptures, Mary absolutely would have made many of these connections.

THE TESTIMONY OF MARY

Upon hearing this wondrous announcement, a jubilant song sprang from Mary's heart. First, she praised and thanked God (vv. 46-50), then she described the Messiah's mission:

> He has scattered those who were proud in the thoughts of their heart.
> He has brought down rulers from their thrones,
> And has exalted those who were humble.
> "He has filled the hungry with good things;
> And sent away the rich empty-handed.
> "He has given help to Israel His servant,
> In remembrance of His mercy,
> As He spoke to our fathers,
> To Abraham and his descendants forever." (vv. 51–56)

Mary's song revolves around two themes. First, she celebrates the age of justice that her son, the Messiah, will usher in. Second, she celebrates the fact that the Messiah will help Israel. Mary's understanding of the mission of the Messiah was thoroughly rooted in her familiarity with the Lord's promises made throughout the Old Testament Scriptures.

THE TESTIMONY OF ZACHARIAS

When Zacharias, the father of John the Baptist, learned that the Messiah was soon to be born, he prophesied under the power of the Holy Spirit:

> "Blessed be the Lord God of Israel, For He has visited us and accomplished redemption for His people, And has raised up a horn of salvation for us in the house of His servant David... Salvation from our enemies... To remember His holy covenant... The oath which He swore to Abraham" (Luke 1:68–73).

What did the Holy Spirit inspire Zacharias to emphasize? Once more, we find a celebration of the Messiah as the son of David, the promised King and deliverer of Israel. The prophecy then celebrates the coming deliverance of Israel from her enemies. Israel will worship the Lord freely, without fear from those who hate them. Zacharias' very Israel-centered expectations are derived entirely from a very straightforward and literal reading of the Lord's promises throughout the Bible of his day.

THE TESTIMONY OF ISRAEL'S FAITHFUL

Luke tells us of others who were also awaiting Israel's redemption: There was Simeon, who was "Righteous and devout, looking for the consolation of Israel" (Luke 2:25). There was Anna, the prophetess, who "began giving thanks to God, and continued to speak of Him to all those who were looking for the redemption of Jerusalem" (Luke 2:38). In the New Testament, those who were devout and holy in Israel are consistently described as waiting for Israel's restoration. Similarly, there was also Joseph of Arimathea, "who was a member of the Council, a good and righteous man... who was waiting for the kingdom of God" (Lk 23:50–51). The Gospels use the terms "consolation of Israel," "redemption of Jerusalem," and "kingdom of God" interchangeably. These faithful Israelites were not misguided. They were filled with the Holy Spirit and steeped in Scripture. Their expectations were correct. Faithful believers today must continue to uphold these same expectations.

ANNA, SIMEON, AND FAITHFUL ISRAEL

THE TESTIMONY FROM HEAVEN

The three gospels of Matthew, Mark, and Luke, all recount that when Jesus was baptized, the voice of God from the heavens declared, "This is My beloved Son, in whom I am well-pleased" (Mt 3:17, cf. Mk 1:11; Lk 3:22). This is another direct allusion to Psalm 2, which begins with the nations in an uproar specifically against YHVH and His Messiah. The Lord's solution to their rebellion is to install His King on Mount Zion (v. 6). The Messiah Himself then declares the words that the Father spoke to Him in heaven:

> "You are My Son, today I have begotten You. Ask of Me, and I will surely give the nations as Your inheritance, and the very ends of the earth as Your possession. You shall break them with a rod of iron, you shall shatter them like earthenware" (vv. 7-9).

A few verses later, the nations are warned to give proper honor where it is due. The kings of the earth are warned to be wise and "kiss the Son" lest His wrath be kindled and they be destroyed in His way (vv. 10–12). Clearly, then, when God the Father spoke from heaven and declared that Jesus of Nazareth was His beloved Son, this would have been understood by everyone present that Jesus is the preexistent Son of God, Messiah, and the Davidic King of Israel.

THE TESTIMONY OF THE MULTITUDES

Many from the crowds who followed Jesus described Him using references from the Hebrew Bible. Many referred to Jesus as "The Prophet," as referred to by Moses in Deuteronomy 18. In the first chapter of the Gospel of John, Philip declared to Nathaniel, "We have found Him of whom Moses in the Law and also the Prophets wrote—Jesus of Nazareth, the son of Joseph" (Jn 1:45). Later, after Jesus had miraculously multiplied the loaves and fish, the crowds declared, "This is truly the Prophet who is to come into the world" (Jn 6:13–14). On yet another occasion, after hearing Jesus speak, the crowds declared, "This certainly is the Prophet" whereas some others were saying, "This is the Christ" (Jn 7:40–41).

Many also referred to Him specifically as "the Son of David." After Jesus healed a demon-possessed man who was blind and mute, "All the crowds were amazed, and were saying, 'This man cannot be the Son of David, can he?'" (Mt 12:22–23). On other occasions, Jesus was referred to as the Son of David by a Canaanite woman, as well as two blind men outside of Jericho (Mt 15:22; 20:29–31). And of course, when Jesus entered Jerusalem just before Passover, "The crowds going ahead of Him, and those who followed, were shouting, 'Hosanna to the Son of David; Blessed is He who comes in the name of the Lord; Hosanna in the highest!'" (Mt 21:9–11). *Hosanna* means "save us!" It is clear that during His ministry, many in Israel believed that Jesus was the prophesied Messiah who had come to save them from their enemies. Nathanael even declared to Jesus, "Rabbi, You are the Son of God; You are the King of Israel" (Jn 1:49). The people of Israel knew the promises that God had given them, and like their forebears, longed for their fulfillment. Do we have these same expectations? Are we also longing for the restoration and consolation of Israel?

THE TESTIMONY OF JESUS DURING HIS MINISTRY

Jesus said many things about Himself, providing us with a clear understanding of how He perceived His own identity and mission. When Pilate asked Jesus if He was indeed the King of the Jews, Jesus answered him, "You say correctly that I am a king. For this I have been born, and for this I have come into the world" (John 18:37). By identifying Himself as the King of the Jews, Jesus was declaring Himself to be the One whom the prophets had foretold.

More than any other term or title, Jesus very purposefully referred to Himself as "the Son of Man." Throughout the four gospels, Jesus refers to Himself by this title 84 times. This was not arbitrary. He believed Himself to be the figure described in Daniel 7, and He wanted everyone else to know it. By repeatedly identifying Himself as the Son of Man,

JESUS DESCRIBES HIS RETURN

THE SIGN OF THE SON OF MAN

Jesus claimed to be both the Messiah and the divine King who would one day receive a kingdom and dominion over all nations. The Son of Man revealed by Daniel must be understood as the fullness of all that the prophets were eagerly awaiting.

Jesus also explicitly referenced His own future enthronement. In Matthew 19:28, He told His disciples:

> "Truly I say to you, that you who have followed Me, in the regeneration, when the Son of Man will sit on His glorious throne, you also shall sit upon twelve thrones, judging the twelve tribes of Israel."

This profound statement reaffirms the Jewish hope in the restoration of the Kingdom of Israel. Jesus envisioned a day when He would be enthroned, and His apostles would reign alongside Him, literally judging the twelve tribes of Israel. There is no hint of allegory here. Jesus was pointing forward to a renewed creation ("the regeneration") in which He would be exalted as King over a restored Israel.

Later, in Matthew 25:31, Jesus again declared:

> "But when the Son of Man comes in His glory, and all the angels with Him, then He will sit on His glorious throne."

This is one of the most majestic self-descriptions Jesus ever uttered. He did not speak of a hidden spiritual rule or an invisible throne in heaven. Instead, He described His return as a glorious cosmic event accompanied by angels, after which He will take His seat upon the throne of His glory to judge the nations. This throne, of course, is none other than the throne of His father David, as promised in Luke 1 and Isaiah 9. These words again echo Daniel 7 and Psalm 2—prophecies of divine enthronement and judgment.

Jesus did not reinterpret the prophecies about Himself—He affirmed them. He did not shift His expectations from a literal kingdom to a purely spiritual one—He confirmed the coming reign of the Messiah in

JESUS DECLARES THE COMING KINGDOM

power and glory. The throne of the Son of Man is the throne of David, and Jesus made it clear that one day, He would sit upon it.

THE TESTIMONY ON THE ROAD TO EMMAUS

After Jesus' death, two very disheartened disciples lamented: "We were hoping that it was He who was going to redeem Israel" (Luke 24:21). Jesus didn't respond by rebuking them for their belief in the restoration of the Kingdom of Israel. He only corrected them for missing the prophecies of the suffering Messiah:

> "Did not the Christ have to suffer these things and then enter His glory?... Beginning with Moses and the Prophets, He explained to them what was said... concerning Himself" (Luke 24:26–27).

Jesus affirmed all that the prophets had spoken. He did not reinterpret or spiritualize their words—He fulfilled them.

CONCLUSION

The testimony of the Gospels is clear: Devout, biblically informed Jews in the New Testament period still clung to the unaltered hope of the Messiah and the restoration of Israel's kingdom. Jesus affirmed this hope. The New Testament does not dismiss or spiritualize God's promises to Israel. Instead, it confirms and builds upon them.

THE EMMAUS ROAD

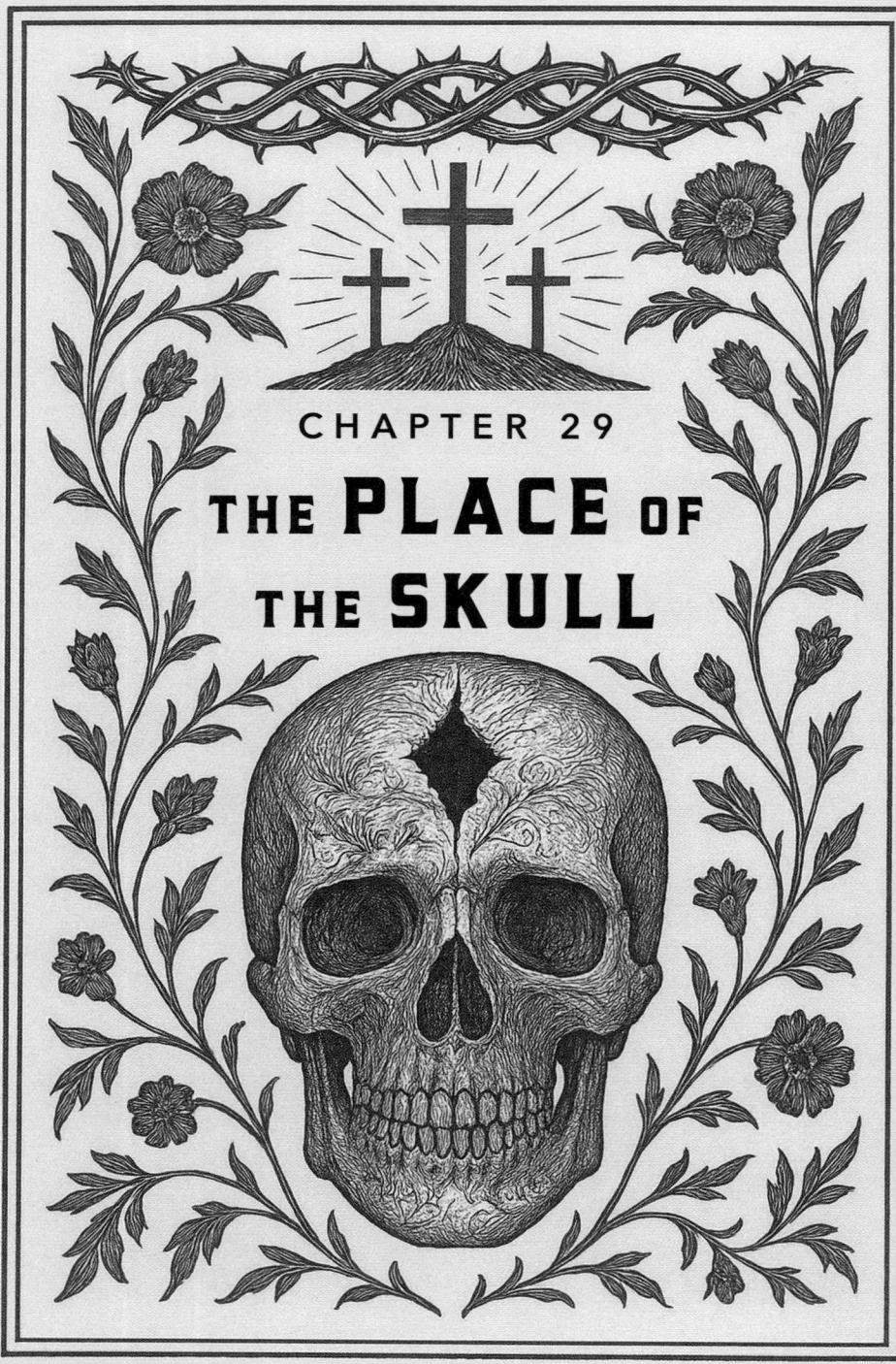

CHAPTER 29

THE PLACE OF THE SKULL

"And when they came to a place called Golgotha, which means Place
  of a Skull..." (Matthew 27:33)

THE GOSPELS TELL US that Jesus was crucified at a location known as
Golgotha—an Aramaic word meaning "The Place of the Skull" (Matt
27:33; John 19:17). While many have speculated that the name came
from the hill's appearance or its use as a place of execution, an ancient
and provocative tradition suggests something even more profound: this
hill may have been the burial site of Goliath's skull.

According to this legend, after David defeated Goliath, he took the
severed head of the giant to Jerusalem—a city that was still controlled
by the Jebusites—and buried it outside the city walls. Scripture seems
to support this:

"David took the head of the Philistine and brought it to Jerusalem,
  but he put his weapons in his tent." (1 Samuel 17:54)

Some early interpreters speculated that David buried Goliath's skull
outside the city, perhaps on a hill that later became known as Golgotha,
which means the Place of the Skull. Some have even suggested that the
etymology of the name Golgotha may specifically refer to Goliath of
Gath (*Gol-Gath-a*). While this story cannot be proven, its symbolic
weight is nonetheless staggering.

Jesus, the greater David, was crucified at the very spot where the skull
of Goliath—the ancient enemy of God's people—was laid to rest. And
it was here, at the *Place of the Skull*, that Jesus delivered the definitive
crushing blow—not to a Philistine warrior, but to Satan himself.

A VIOLENT VICTORY

From Genesis 3:15 onward, Scripture describes a war between two
seeds—the seed of the woman and the seed of the serpent. The promise
was that one day, the Seed of the woman would come, and though His
heel would be struck, He would crush the head of the serpent, forever.

DAVID BRINGS GOLIATH'S HEAD TO JERUSALEM

That promise was guaranteed not in a battle, but on a cross. Jesus' crucifixion was not the tragedy of a failed prophet—it was the triumph of the Skull Crusher. As His hands and feet were pierced and His side opened, His heel was struck—but through His resurrection, the serpent's head was shattered. The crucifixion site became the ultimate battlefield, where the Son of David took down the greatest enemy of all.

Throughout our journey, we've traced how the Messiah is not only the Seed of the Woman, but also the Cloud Rider of Sinai, the Rock that Crushes, and the Son of Man who rides on the clouds. He is the Tent Peg, the Star of Jacob, the Branch, the Servant, the Shepherd, and the Coming King. Nowhere do all of those identities converge more powerfully than at Golgotha. There, the Skull Crusher became the Crucified One, and by His wounds, He purchased the nations. The Seed of the woman suffered—but in that suffering, He conquered.

The place of the skull is where death was defeated.

Golgotha was not just a hill outside Jerusalem—it was the cosmic arena where Christ disarmed the powers and authorities, made a public spectacle of them, and triumphed over them by the cross (Col 2:15). Jesus' final words on the cross, "It is finished," were not words of defeat. They were the shout of a victorious warrior.

THE WAR IS OVER—BUT THE MARCH CONTINUES

The Skull Crusher has come. But He will come again. He came once to defeat sin, but He will come again to finish what He guaranteed. At the cross, Jesus struck the decisive blow against Satan. It was not the final act in the war, but it was the turning point—the moment the outcome was guaranteed. Satan was spiritually and legally disarmed (Colossians 2:15); his hold over humanity was broken (Hebrews 2:14); and his final judgment was sealed. From that moment forward, his doom is only a matter of time.

At the cross, the serpent's head was crushed in principle. Still, after Jesus returns, it will be crushed to the full when Satan is cast into the lake of fire (Revelation 20:10). The victory has already been won, but the final mop-up operation is still ahead.

GOLGOTHA

Next we turn to the book of Acts, where Jesus' disciples were commissioned to go into all the world, declaring His victory, making disciples, and preparing the nations for the return of the King. The war was won at Golgotha, but the campaign to announce the victory had only just begun.

The place of the skull was the pivot point of history. From it flowed redemption, healing, and hope. And it was there, perhaps where the severed head of Goliath lay symbolically beneath the cross, that the final giant of sin and death was defeated.

GOLGOTHA

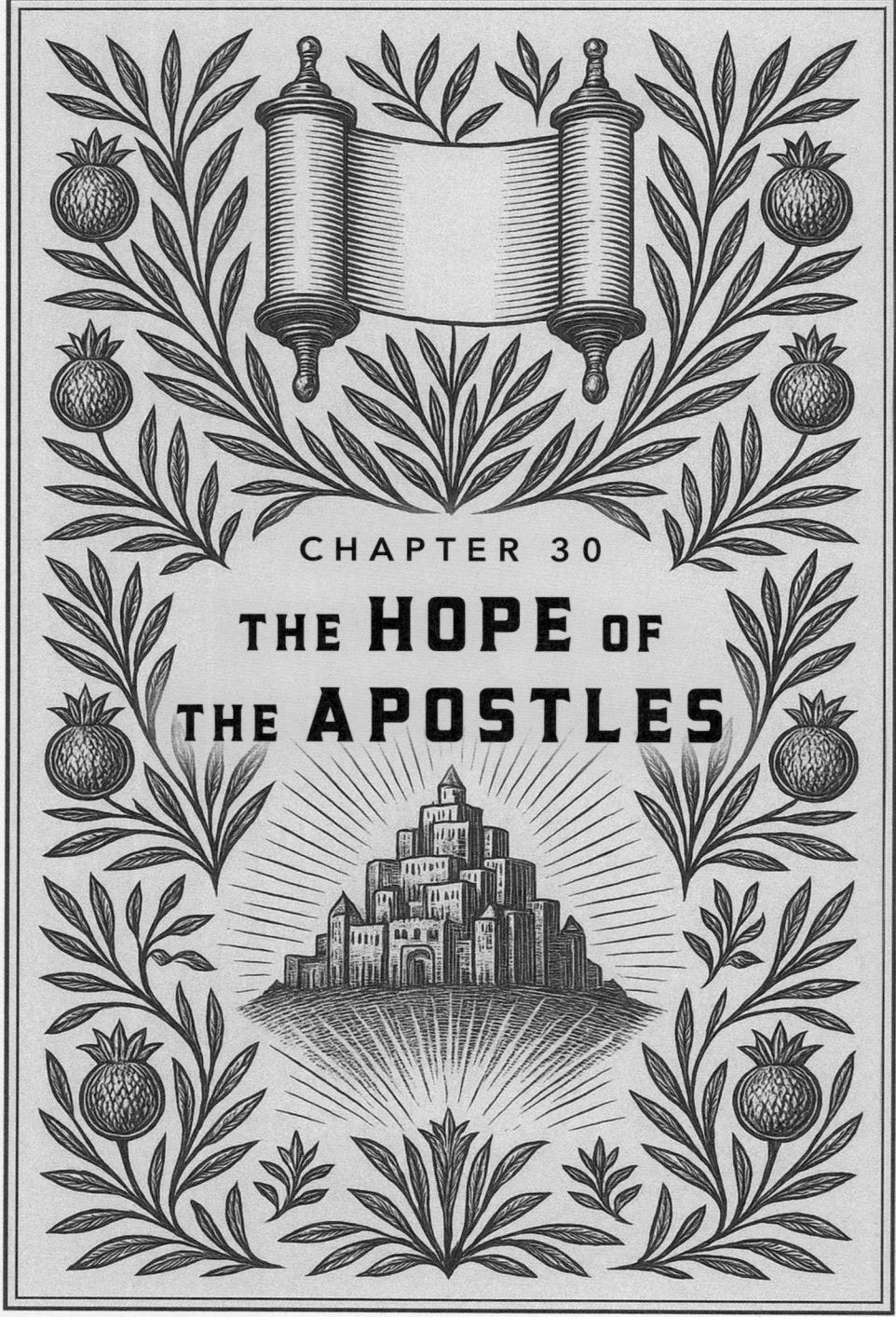

CHAPTER 30

THE **HOPE** OF **THE APOSTLES**

THE BOOK OF THE ACTS OF THE APOSTLES opens with a truly stunning account of Jesus' interaction with His disciples after the resurrection. First, it tells us that He appeared to them over a period of forty days and taught them about the Kingdom of God:

> "To these He also presented Himself alive after His suffering, by many convincing proofs, appearing to them over a period of forty days and speaking of the things concerning the kingdom of God" (Acts 1:3).

Imagine sitting in on a private Bible study, personally taught by the resurrected, glorified Jesus. That is precisely what happened. The subject of His teaching was specifically: "the Kingdom of God." This is why their next question is so important. They asked Him, "Lord, is it at this time You are restoring the kingdom to Israel?" (Acts 1:6). To the disciples, "the Kingdom of God" and the restored "Kingdom of Israel" were the same thing. Their question was a very natural and logical question for anyone who had grown up studying the Scriptures. Jesus answered them accordingly:

> "It is not for you to know times or epochs which the Father has fixed by His own authority; but you will receive power when the Holy Spirit has come upon you; and you shall be My witnesses both in Jerusalem, and in all Judea and Samaria, and even to the remotest part of the earth." (Acts 1:7–8)

Notice that Jesus did not rebuke or correct them. He didn't say, "You've misunderstood the kingdom." Instead, He told them that the timing was not for them to know. He repeated what He had already taught before His crucifixion: "Of that day and hour no one knows, not even the angels of heaven, nor the Son, but the Father alone" (Matt. 24:36).

Jesus then instructed them to stay in Jerusalem and wait for the promised Holy Spirit (Acts 1:5). The Spirit would empower them to proclaim the future, coming kingdom, just as He had done during His earthly ministry.

JESUS TEACHES ON THE KINGDOM FOR FORTY DAYS

JESUS' VISIBLE RETURN

Next, the disciples watched as Jesus ascended into the sky:

> "...and a cloud received Him out of their sight" (Acts 1:9). As they gazed upward, two angels appeared and said, "Men of Galilee, why do you stand looking into the sky? This Jesus, who has been taken up from you into heaven, will come in just the same way as you have watched Him go" (Acts 1:10–11).

Before their very eyes, Jesus visibly ascended into the clouds and disappeared. The angels promised that He would return in the same manner, visibly and in the clouds. Just as the Old Testament consistently teaches that the Promised One will someday come from heaven in the clouds, so does the New Testament consistently teach that Jesus will return in the clouds, in radiant glory, visibly, for all to see. Jesus Himself declared: "...they will see the Son of Man coming on the clouds of the sky with power and great glory" (Matt. 24:30). The Book of Revelation declares "Behold, He is coming with the clouds, and every eye will see Him, even those who pierced Him..." (Rev. 1:7). Later, when some were teaching that Jesus had already spiritually returned, Paul stated emphatically that they had "gone astray from the faith" (1 Tim. 6:20–21). Denying the visible, future return of Jesus is not a minor error—it's a denial of biblical faith, a denial of the Christian faith. As both the Apostles' and Nicene Creeds declare: "He will come again in glory to judge the living and the dead." To reject a future, visible return of Jesus is to reject both the consistent teachings of Scripture and the ancient historical creeds of the Christian faith.

PETER'S FIRST SERMON AFTER PENTECOST

After Jesus ascended into heaven and sat down at the right hand of God, after the Holy Spirit had fallen on the disciples, they continued to bear witness concerning the future restoration of the throne of David:

THE ASCENSION

"Brethren, I may confidently say to you regarding the patriarch David that he both died and was buried, and his tomb is with us to this day. And so, because he was a prophet and knew that God had sworn to him with an oath to seat one of his descendants on his throne, he looked ahead and spoke of the resurrection of the Christ, that He was neither abandoned to Hades, nor did His flesh suffer decay. This Jesus God raised up again, to which we are all witnesses. (Acts 2:29-32).

Peter alluded to two passages. The first is Psalm 16:10, in which David declares that the Lord would not let His "holy one" remain in the grave or see decay. The second is the Davidic Covenant (2 Sam 7:12-13), in which God promised David a descendant who would sit on His throne forever. Peter sought to prove that Jesus was the Messiah. David died after all, and his body had decayed. Thus, David was not speaking about himself, but the Messiah, whom the Lord would raise from the dead. For what purpose did the Lord raise Jesus up? To sit on David's throne. Peter thus continued his argument by quoting Psalm 110:

"For it was not David who ascended into heaven, but he himself says: 'The Lord said to my Lord, "Sit at My right hand, Until I make Your enemies a footstool for Your feet."

Peter then completes his argument by declaring:

"Therefore let all the house of Israel know for certain that God has made Him both Lord and Christ—this Jesus whom you crucified." (Acts 2:34–36)

Psalm 110 teaches that after ascending, the Messiah would sit at God's right hand until the appointed time for Him to crush His enemies under His feet. The acts of reestablishing David's throne and crushing Israel's enemies are synonymous. Peter's point is simple: Jesus is the One who didn't remain in the grave (Ps 16:10), He is the One who is now at the right hand of the Father (Ps 110), and will remain there until the time comes for Him to come back, reestablish the throne of David (2 Sam 7), and crush the wicked kings and the rebellious from among the nations (Ps 110: 5-6).

PETER'S SECOND SERMON

Peter's second sermon reinforces all of the same truths. To his countrymen, Peter shouted aloud:

> "Therefore repent and return, so that your sins may be wiped away, in order that times of refreshing may come… and that He may send Jesus, the Christ appointed for you, whom heaven must receive until the period of restoration of all things…" (Acts 3:19–21)

Peter called His people to repentance, for the forgiveness of their sins. But Jesus, he declared, will remain in heaven until the time for the restoration of all things—namely, the restoration of Eden, the restoration of David's throne, Israel's kingdom, and ultimately, the entire earth. This is the consistent message of the entire Bible. It is for this very reason that Peter says that this time of refreshing or period of restoration is that "which God spoke by the mouth of His holy prophets from ancient time." (v. 21). This is simply Peter's way of saying that this is the consistent message of the entire Bible.

THE JERUSALEM COUNCIL: THE FALLEN TENT OF DAVID

One of the most significant moments in the early Church occurred at the Jerusalem Council, as recorded in Acts 15. As the apostles debated the question of whether Gentile believers needed to be circumcised and keep the Law of Moses to be saved, after prayerfully seeking the wisdom of the Holy Spirit, James—leader of the Jerusalem church—stood up and gave his judgment. In doing so, he quoted a powerful messianic prophecy from Amos:

JAMES PREACHES AT JERUSALEM COUNCIL

"After these things I will return, And I will rebuild the tabernacle of David which has fallen, And I will rebuild its ruins, And I will restore it, So that the rest of mankind may seek the Lord, And all the Gentiles who are called by My name." (Acts 15:16–17)

James cited this passage to affirm what was taking place before their very eyes: the Gentiles were indeed turning to Israel's God through Jesus the Messiah. But he also made it clear that what they were witnessing was not the *final or ultimate* fulfillment of Amos's prophecy. It was the beginning stages of it. James still speaks of a future "return." The complete restoration of David's fallen tent—the royal house and throne of David—is yet to come.

This quotation from Amos echoes everything the prophets had declared. The "tent of David" was not just a poetic phrase—it referred to the Davidic monarchy, the very throne promised to the Messiah. What James is doing here is incredibly important. He affirms that the inclusion of the Gentiles was always part of the prophetic plan. He never redefines or spiritualizes the restoration of David's kingdom. Instead, he confirms its future fulfillment. First, the Gentiles are gathered in, then the King returns to restore David's throne.

This places the Church—not as a replacement for Israel—but as the first-fruits of the coming Kingdom, a foretaste of what is yet to come when Jesus reigns from Zion and rules the whole world (Isaiah 2:2–4). The promises remain intact. The hope is still alive. And the apostles were careful stewards of that expectation.

PAUL'S CONSISTENT MESSAGE

From the outset of his ministry to the very end of his life, the Apostle Paul boldly preached the same hope—the future restoration of Israel and the coming Messianic Kingdom. His message never changed. In Ephesus, we're told he spent three months in the synagogue, "reasoning and persuading them about the kingdom of God" (Acts 19:8). Later, in Asia, Luke says Paul "went about preaching the kingdom" (Acts 20:25). Whether among

Jews or Gentiles, Paul's proclamation remained focused on the same central theme. When Paul was on trial before Agrippa, he testified:

> "And now I am standing trial for the hope of the promise made by God to our fathers; the promise to which our twelve tribes hope to attain, as they earnestly serve God night and day" (Acts 26:6–7).

This statement is so crucial that it bears citing twice. Please read it slowly: "the hope of the promise made by God to our fathers; the promise to which our twelve tribes hope to attain." This was not some abstract spiritual hope—it was the specific promise of the restoration of the kingdom, the fulfillment of everything the prophets had spoken, the very hope of Israel itself. This is why, as Acts draws to a close, Paul tells the Jewish leaders in Rome:

> "I requested to see you and to speak with you, since I am wearing this chain for the sake of the hope of Israel" (Acts 28:20).

That hope is the same hope he'd proclaimed from the beginning of his ministry. Paul continued to teach and testify about Jesus from the Law and the Prophets, proclaiming the coming Kingdom of God just as Jesus had taught (Acts 28:23). Luke ends Acts by declaring:

> "He stayed two full years in his own rented lodging and welcomed all who came to him, preaching the kingdom of God and teaching things about the Lord Jesus Christ with all openness, unhindered" (Acts 28:30–31).

Paul's final words in the book are not abstract or philosophical. He continues to preach the kingdom of God, rooted in the covenants, the prophets, and the hope of Israel. This is no spiritualized kingdom here. It is the same literal, future kingdom that all the prophets of Israel foresaw and all the righteous of Israel longed for. For Paul, Jesus was—and remains—the fulfillment and embodiment of that promise.

ONE UNIFIED HOPE

From the first chapter of Acts to the last, the apostolic message never changed. It remained anchored in the concrete expectation of Jesus' visible return and the restoration of the Kingdom to Israel. Whether it was Peter, James, Stephen, or Paul, each of them affirmed the same hope that had been proclaimed since the beginning—through the Torah, the Psalms, and the Prophets. They declared what had already been revealed. The inclusion of the Gentiles was never seen as a replacement of Israel but as a fulfillment of the promise that through Abraham's seed all nations would be blessed. The apostolic Church saw itself not as the end of God's story with Israel but as its beginning—a firstfruits community awaiting the return of the King and the final restoration of all things. This is the hope that drove the apostles. This is the hope that frames the entire New Testament. And this is the hope that has been proclaimed throughout the entire Bible.

IN CHAINS FOR THE HOPE OF ISRAEL

CHAPTER 31

THE BLESSED HOPE

THE EPISTLES OF THE NEW TESTAMENT—LETTERS written by the apostles to early churches and individuals—are most often seen as rich in doctrine, practical wisdom, and ethical exhortations. But woven throughout these pastoral letters is an unwavering hope in the return of Jesus and the establishment of His future kingdom on the earth. The epistles do not teach that the Kingdom has already come. Instead, they point forward with eager longing to the day when Jesus will reign visibly from Zion, the nations will be judged in righteousness, and the age of restoration will finally come.

A FORWARD-FACING GOSPEL

The apostolic gospel—the primary message that Paul and the other writers proclaim—is not merely a message about the forgiveness of sins but also of Jesus as the risen and exalted Messiah who will return. Paul opens his letter to the Romans by describing the gospel as concerning:

> "His Son, who was born of a descendant of David according to the flesh, who was declared the Son of God with power by the resurrection from the dead" (Romans 1:3–4).

How would anyone who knew the Scriptures interpret such a statement? This is the seed of David, the promised King.

Though Jesus has ascended to the right hand of God, His earthly messianic reign over the nations remains in the future. Paul reminds the Corinthian church that Christ "must reign until" the time comes when He will crush "His enemies under His feet" (1 Cor. 15:25). The consummation of all things will come when He "delivers up the kingdom to the God and Father" (v. 24). In Paul's day, this was not something that had already happened, and even today, we eagerly await its fulfillment.

THE HOPE OF HIS APPEARING

The apostles consistently speak of awaiting a second, climactic coming of Jesus. Paul writes to Titus that believers are to live "sensibly, righteously,

CRUSHING HIS ENEMIES

and godly in the present age, looking for the blessed hope and the appearing of the glory of our great God and Savior, Christ Jesus" (Titus 2:13). This "appearing" is not some invisible, secret event, but His future, visible, and glorious appearing when He comes back in the clouds, accompanied by an army of holy ones.

In his letters to Timothy, Paul echoes this hope repeatedly. He charges Timothy to "keep the commandment without stain or reproach until the appearing of our Lord Jesus Christ" (1 Tim. 6:14). Near the end of his life, he speaks of the "crown of righteousness" laid up for him, "and not only to me, but also to all who have loved His appearing" (2 Tim. 4:8). The hope of Jesus' return is not incidental to Paul's letters—it is the very heart of all Christian longing.

JUDGMENT AND VINDICATION

The return of Jesus is also described as the day of righteous judgment. To the Thessalonians, Paul writes that "the Lord Jesus will be revealed from heaven with His mighty angels in flaming fire, dealing out retribution to those who do not know God" (2 Thess. 1:7–8). The same Jesus who was rejected and crucified will return as Judge, vindicating His name and rewarding the afflicted.

This judgment includes not only the defeat of wicked individuals but of all systems of rebellion. Paul refers to the last great rebel: "the man of lawlessness" (2 Thess. 2:3–4), whom "the Lord will slay with the breath of His mouth and bring to an end by the appearance of His coming" (v. 8). Echoing Daniel and Ezekiel's vision of the final beast, Paul identifies the Antichrist figure as the culmination of satanic deception, destined for destruction when the Messiah comes in power.

INHERITING THE KINGDOM

James calls believers "heirs of the kingdom" (Jas. 2:5). The kingdom is promised to those who persevere in faith and suffering. Paul and Barnabas encouraged early believers by saying, "Through many tribulations we must enter the kingdom of God" (Acts 14:22). If we are suffering now, it is because the kingdom is not yet here.

Paul's emphasis on the resurrection (especially in 1 Corinthians 15) is tied directly to kingdom hope. He makes it clear that sinful, corrupt, mortal "flesh and blood cannot inherit the kingdom of God" (1 Cor. 15:50). It is only through resurrection—when the dead are raised imperishable and mortality puts on immortality—that believers can enter the kingdom. Thus, the kingdom awaits the resurrection, which itself awaits the return of the King.

THE ROYAL SON AND THE DAY OF GLORY

The epistles also affirm Jesus' Davidic identity. Paul, Peter, and James all speak of Jesus in ways that reflect the messianic promises made to David. Jesus is called the "Son of David" (2 Tim. 2:8), and His return is defined as the moment when "every knee will bow" (Phil. 2:10), and the nations will acknowledge Him as Lord.

Nowhere do the apostles say that the kingdom is present. Instead, they urge believers to wait patiently, to endure suffering, and to fix their hope on the day when Jesus will be revealed. "Our citizenship is in heaven," Paul says, "from which we also eagerly wait for a Savior, the Lord Jesus Christ" (Phil. 3:20). He will come not to rule from heaven, but to "transform the body of our humble state into conformity with the body of His glory" (v. 21)—a bodily, visible change that accompanies the dawn of the kingdom age.

THE ENDURANCE OF THE SAINTS

The Book of Hebrews offers some of the most passionate exhortations in the New Testament to persevere in light of the coming kingdom. In chapters 10 through 12, the author calls believers to endure suffering and remain faithful, knowing that the promises of God have not yet been fulfilled but are surely coming. The author of Hebrews writes, "You have need of endurance, so that when you have done the will of God, you may receive what was promised" (Heb. 10:36).

What was promised is not simply spiritual comfort or inner peace—it is the arrival of the promised kingdom, the day when the Messiah

THE LADDER OF FAITHFUL ENDURANCE

THE ANCHOR OF HOPE

returns and restores all things. Quoting from Habakkuk, the author declares: "For yet in a very little while, He who is coming will come, and will not delay" (Heb. 10:37).

Through the letter to the Hebrews, the faithful are those who live not for this present age, but for the world to come. They are like the heroes of faith in chapter 11—men and women who embraced the promises of God from afar and "died in faith, without receiving the promises, but having seen them and having welcomed them from a distance" (Heb. 11:13). These saints understood that the fulfillment was yet future. So they lived accordingly, waiting patiently in hope.

As an earlier exhortation states, the good news concerning the coming Kingdom is "the hope set before us," describing it as "a sure and steadfast anchor of the soul" (Heb. 6:18–19). In keeping with this theme, Hebrews 12 appeals to all believers to "run with endurance the race that is set before us, fixing our eyes on Jesus... who for the joy set before Him endured the cross" (Heb. 12:1–2). That same joy, the coming glory and restoration of all things, is the prize held out before us.

Hebrews confirms everything the prophets, Jesus, and the apostles have declared: the kingdom is coming, and those who endure in faith will inherit it. Until then, we wait—not passively, but faithfully—pressing on toward Zion, the city of the living God (Heb. 12:22–24), where Jesus reigns as both our King and our eternal High Priest. He is our anchor of hope—both steadfast and sure.

LONGING

The epistles are filled with longing. They do not proclaim a kingdom already established but a kingdom that will come in power and glory. They testify of a Messiah who has been exalted to the Father's right hand, to wait until the appointed time when He will return and crush His enemies underfoot. They speak of the glorious appearing of the Son of Man, a day of judgment, a resurrection of the righteous, and the establishment of His eternal throne on the earth. The messianic hope of the prophets and apostles is the same. And it remains the hope of all who have loved His appearing.

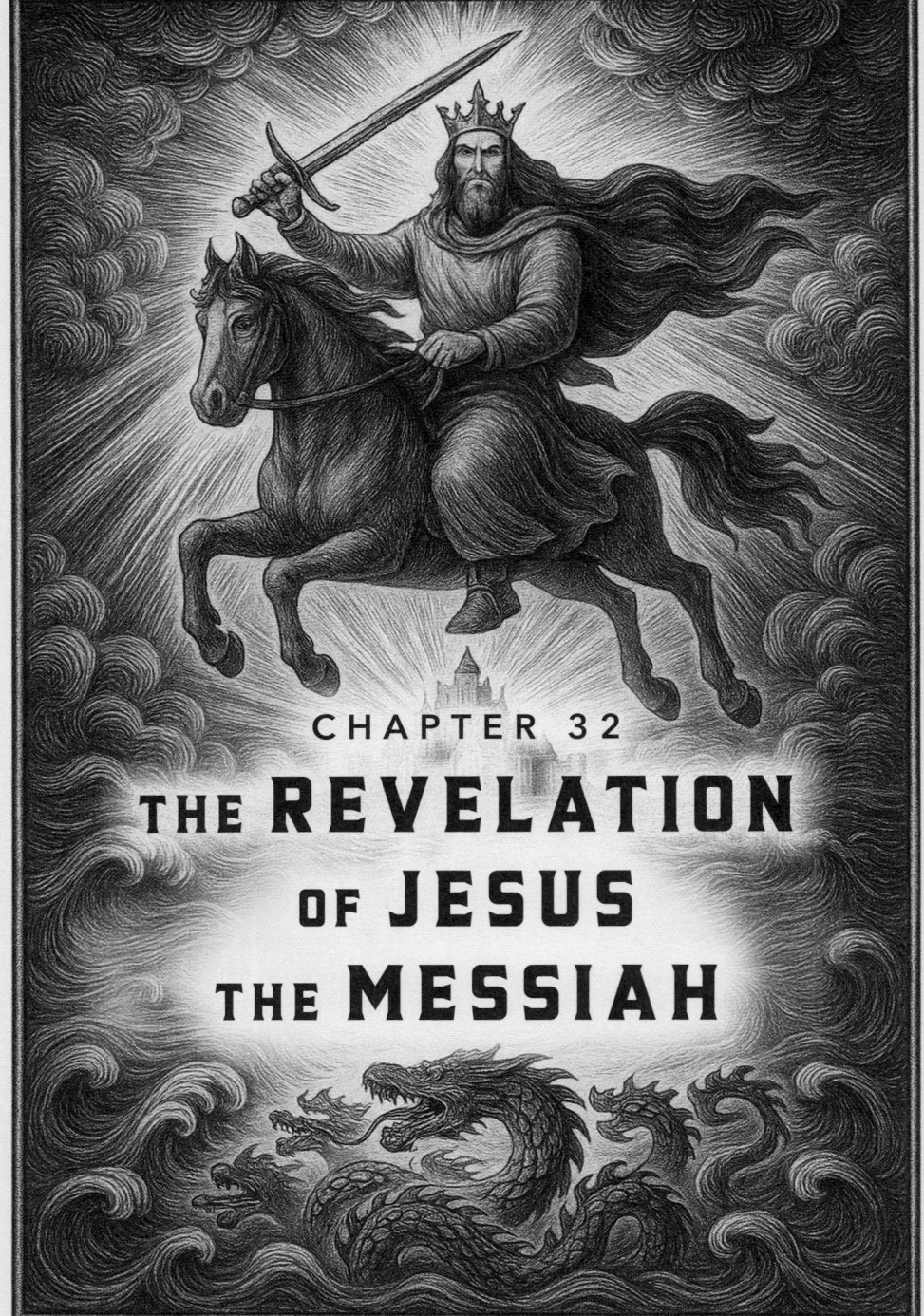

CHAPTER 32

THE REVELATION OF JESUS THE MESSIAH

THE BOOK OF GENESIS opens with the promise of the Skull Crusher, and the book of Revelation closes with His arrival. From beginning to end, the Scriptures tell one great drama—the restoration of all things under the reign of Jesus the Messiah. Every symbol, every promise, every name, and every covenant have been building to this final crescendo: the return of the King, the triumph of the Lamb, and the crushing of the serpent and the beast once and for all.

The book of Revelation is not merely a cryptic prophecy full of strange symbols or a speculative timeline for the last days. It is a divine unveiling. It reveals Jesus in His full glory—the conquering King, the Lamb upon the throne, the Judge of the nations, and the fulfillment of every messianic promise. It is ultimately a letter written to a people under pressure and persecution, reminding them to endure patiently and faithfully, because their King is coming soon.

THE LION AND THE LAMB

In Revelation 5, John sees a scroll sealed with seven seals. But no one is found worthy to open it, and so John the Apostle begins to weep. Then one of the elders says to him:

> "Weep no more; behold, the Lion of the tribe of Judah, the Root of David, has conquered, so that he can open the scroll and its seven seals" (Revelation 5:5).

Look at these words. This is the fulfillment of Jacob's ancient blessing in Genesis 49. The scepter would not depart from Judah. After millennia of waiting, the Lion King will finally rule. But when John turns to see this Lion, he sees a Lamb, standing as though it had been slain. The conquering King is also the slain Lamb. The Skull Crusher is also the Suffering Servant and the Crucified One. In this paradox lies the heart of the gospel: Jesus conquered not by taking life, but by laying down His own. He overcame by being overcome. By willingly allowing Himself to be struck, He sealed the serpent's fate. And now, His victory at the cross will give way to His visible reign over all nations.

THE ALPHA AND OMEGA

THE LION AND LAMB

THE ONE WHO TREADS THE WINEPRESS

Throughout this study, we've traced the hope of a coming King who would destroy the wicked, vindicate the righteous, and rule in righteousness. In Revelation 19, the King finally appears. Heaven opens, and the Rider on the white horse descends:

> "From His mouth comes a sharp sword with which to strike down the nations, and He will rule them with a rod of iron. He will tread the winepress of the fury of the wrath of God the Almighty" (Revelation 19:15).

This is not the meek and lowly Jesus of His first coming. This is the King of kings and Lord of lords. Reflecting imagery that we've already seen, His robe is dipped in blood—the blood of His enemies. He treads the winepress, crushing the rebellious nations like grapes underfoot. This scene recalls Isaiah 63, where the Messiah comes from Bozrah, garments stained with blood, having trampled the peoples in judgment. It is also the fulfillment of Psalm 2, where the Son is given the nations as His inheritance and crushes them with a rod of iron.

The One who was crushed has now become the Crusher.

THE BEAST AND THE DRAGON DESTROYED

Just as Genesis introduces the serpent who deceives and devours, Revelation concludes with his final judgment. In chapter 19, after the appearance of the King, we read:

> "And the beast was captured, and with it the false prophet... These two were thrown alive into the lake of fire that burns with sulfur" (Revelation 19:20).

This is the long-awaited downfall of the beast—the satanically empowered empire and its counterfeit messiah. Throughout the Bible, the beast has devoured, deceived, and warred against the saints. But now

REVELATION 19

the tables are turned. The throne of man has been shattered. The lies of Antichrist are silenced forever. Immediately following, in Revelation 20, the dragon—identified as the ancient serpent, the devil, and Satan—is also judged:

> "And the devil who had deceived them was thrown into the lake of fire and sulfur... and they will be tormented day and night forever and ever" (Revelation 20:10).

Genesis 3:15 has finally been fulfilled. The Seed of the woman has crushed the serpent's head. The great adversary of God and man is no more. No more deception. No more rebellion. No more accusations. The serpent is crushed. The dragon and the beast are destroyed, and the war is over.

THE RAINBOW ANGEL

Before the final trumpet sounds, Revelation 10 introduces us to a majestic figure:

> "I saw another strong angel coming down out of heaven, clothed with a cloud; and the rainbow was upon his head, and his face was like the sun, and his feet like pillars of fire" (Revelation 10:1).

Though some interpret this angel as a high-ranking heavenly messenger, the imagery suggests otherwise. He is clothed with a cloud. A rainbow surrounds His head. His face shines like the sun. His feet blaze like fire. All of this imagery ties this glorious One. He has attributes of both YHVH and the Angel of the Lord from the Exodus. He sets one foot on the sea and one on the land, declaring dominion over all creation, possibly indicating His splitting of the sea once again. Then, He roars like a lion, swearing that "there will be delay no longer." The mystery of God is about to be completed. The Exodus imagery is thick: clouds, fire, thunder, scrolls, and parting seas. The Lion is about to roar. The final Exodus is about to begin.

THE MIGHTY ANGEL

THE NEW JERUSALEM: EDEN RESTORED

As Babylon falls, the new Jerusalem descends. A city adorned like a bride for her husband. The home of the righteous is not an escape to heaven, but the arrival of heaven to earth.

> "Behold, the dwelling place of God is with man. He will dwell with them, and they will be His people... He will wipe away every tear from their eyes" (Revelation 21:3–4).

The throne of God and of the Lamb is there. The river of life flows there. The tree of life bearing fruit for the healing of the nations is freely accessible once again. The curse is gone. The serpent is gone. Eden has been restored.

THE FINAL WORD

The author of Hebrews describes Jesus as "a sure and steadfast anchor of the soul, a hope that enters into the inner place behind the curtain" (Hebrews 6:19). The book of Revelation shows us what lies beyond that curtain. The hope that anchors our souls is no longer veiled. The revelation from heaven has finally arrived. The word "Revelation" means unveiling. This final book of Scripture pulls back the veil not only on future events but on the identity of Jesus Himself:

He is the Seed of the Woman who crushes the serpent. He is the Son of David who rules the nations. He is the Lamb who was slain. He is the Lion of Judah. He is the Cloud Rider. He is the Angel of the Exodus. He is the Rock that crushes. He is the Judge who treads the winepress. As the book comes to a close, we can hear His resounding promise: "Surely I am coming soon" (Revelation 22:20). To which the Church in unison replies:

"Maranatha. Come, Lord Jesus!"

PARADISE RESTORED

CHAPTER 33

THE ENTRANCE TO THE KINGDOM

WE'VE COMPLETED OUR JOURNEY. Together, we've followed the golden thread of God's unfolding promise-plan from Genesis to Revelation. We've traced the story of redemption as the Bible tells it, rich with vibrant, visceral metaphors. We've allowed ourselves to be swept up in the beauty of a story still unfolding even now on the world stage. It is the story of Jesus, who suffered, died, rose again, ascended into heaven, and who will return in blazing fire to slay the dragon, judge the wicked, restore the Kingdom to Israel, and reign as King over the whole earth.

This Kingdom—marked by justice, righteousness, peace, and joy—will never end. But one critical question remains:

How do we enter this Kingdom?

HOPE FOR THE HOPELESS

Isaiah 59 offers a direct and sobering diagnosis of the human condition. The problem isn't with God, but with us:

> "Behold, the Lord's hand is not so short that it cannot save; Nor is His ear so dull that it cannot hear. But your iniquities have made a separation between you and your God, And your sins have hidden His face from you so that He does not hear." (Isaiah 59:1–2)

We are all sinners, and our sin separates us from God. Isaiah describes a people lost in rebellion and injustice. Truth has stumbled. Righteousness stands far off. No one is righteous—not even one.

Yet in our helplessness, God intervenes. He sends His Redeemer:

> "A Redeemer will come to Zion, and to those who turn from transgression in Jacob," declares the Lord. "As for Me, this is My covenant with them," says the Lord: "My Spirit which is upon you, and My words which I have put in your mouth shall not depart from your mouth, nor from the mouth of your offspring, nor from the mouth of your offspring's offspring," says the Lord, "from now and forever." (Isaiah 59:20–21)

This is the New Covenant. When the Redeemer comes to Zion, God offers both forgiveness and transformation. He gives His own Spirit, teaching and empowering us to walk in His ways.

Jeremiah expands on this promise:

> "Behold, days are coming," declares the Lord, "when I will make a new covenant with the house of Israel and with the house of Judah—not like the covenant I made with their fathers... My covenant which they broke... But this is the covenant I will make... I will put My law within them and write it on their heart; and I will be their God, and they shall be My people... for I will forgive their iniquity, and their sin I will remember no more." (Jeremiah 31:31–34)

Unlike the Mosaic covenant—broken repeatedly—this one is internal. God writes His law on hearts. He forgives, restores, and indwells. Ezekiel echoes the same:

> "I will sprinkle clean water on you, and you will be clean... I will give you a new heart and put a new spirit within you... I will put My Spirit within you and cause you to walk in My statutes... You will be My people, and I will be your God." (Ezekiel 36:25–28)

This is the essence of the New Covenant: cleansing, a new heart, and the indwelling Spirit. To enter the Kingdom, the King must place His Spirit within us and give us His heart.

THE MESSIAH IS THE COVENANT

Isaiah adds a profound truth—not only will the Messiah bring a covenant, He *is* the covenant:

> "I will appoint You as a covenant to the people, as a light to the nations." (Isaiah 42:6; cf. 49:8)

Isaiah, Jeremiah, and Ezekiel looked forward to the day when this covenant would come. The good news is that the mediator of this better covenant has already arrived. Jesus is the New Covenant in person.

At the Last Supper, He lifted the cup and declared:

"This cup is the new covenant in My blood, which is poured out for you." (Luke 22:20)

The Suffering Servant has already said, "It is finished." The door to this covenant is now open.

THE HOLY SPIRIT

John's Gospel records a nighttime conversation between Jesus and Nicodemus, a leading teacher of Israel. Jesus was astonished that Nicodemus didn't understand the need to be "born of the Spirit" to enter the Kingdom. After all, the prophets had spoken so clearly about the New Covenant and the giving of God's Spirit. Whether we call it being "born again" or "entering the New Covenant," the meaning is the same. Jesus described this as a second birth—a spiritual birth. When we turn from sin and return to God (*teshuva* in Hebrew), we are born again. We receive the Spirit of adoption, entering into an intimate familial relationship with God and gaining the power to walk faithfully before Him.

REPENT AND BELIEVE

It all begins with *teshuva*—repentance. It means turning from sin, rebellion, and self-reliance, and turning to God and Jesus, His Messiah. We trust that the Messiah came, died for our sins, and rose again, according to the Scriptures. As Paul says:

"If you confess with your mouth Jesus as Lord, and believe in your heart that God raised Him from the dead, you will be saved; for with the heart a person believes, resulting in righteousness, and with the mouth he confesses, resulting in salvation." (Romans 10:9–10)

NICODEMUS AND JESUS

And Peter proclaimed:

> "Repent, and let each of you be baptized in the name of Jesus Christ for the forgiveness of your sins; and you shall receive the gift of the Holy Spirit." (Acts 2:38)

And of course, most are pretty familiar with John 3:16:

> "For God so loved the world, that He gave His only begotten Son, that whoever believes in Him shall not perish, but have eternal life."

And as Jesus told Martha:

> "I am the resurrection and the life; he who believes in Me will live even if he dies, and everyone who lives and believes in Me will never die. Do you believe this?" (John 11:25–26)

Over and over, Scripture declares:

> "Everyone who believes in Him..." "Whoever trusts in Him..." "All who believe..." "For whoever will call upon the name of the Lord will be saved." (Romans 10:13)

OBEY AND ENDURE

Trusting Jesus isn't merely a one-time act—it's a whole-life response. As we turn away from sin, we choose to obey His righteous ways. As Jesus said:

> "If you love Me, you will keep My commandments." (John 14:15)

We're not saved *by* obedience, but true faith is shown *through* obedience. The Holy Spirit empowers us to live faithfully *to the end*. Entering the Kingdom is the beginning of a difficult journey. Jesus said many will finish strong. It requires daily self-denial and endurance. He warned:

BORN OF THE SPIRIT

"The one who endures to the end, he will be saved." (Matthew 24:13)

The author of Hebrews urges us to:

"Run with endurance the race that is set before us, fixing our eyes on Jesus." (Hebrews 12:1–2)

The narrow road of discipleship is often painful and costly. But Jesus promised:

"The one who overcomes will inherit these things, and I will be his God and he will be My son." (Revelation 21:7)

To help us endure, God gives the Holy Spirit, who leads, reminds, and strengthens us. As Paul told the Colossians:

"Continue in the faith, firmly established and steadfast, and not moved away from the hope of the gospel." (Colossians 1:23)

AN INVITATION

If you haven't yet turned to God, I invite you now. If you've not yet entered the New Covenant, the door is wide open. Scripture says:

"Whoever will call upon the name of the Lord will be saved." (Romans 10:13)

"And let the one who is thirsty come; let the one who wishes take the water of life without cost." (Revelation 22:17)

This is God's offer of forgiveness, cleansing, renewal, and eternal life. It's not just an invitation—it's an appeal to bow the knee before the King returns to judge the living and the dead:

JESUS IS THE DOOR

"He who testifies to these things says, 'Yes, I am coming quickly.' Amen. Come, Lord Jesus." (Revelation 22:20)

So come. Bow your knee to the coming King. Enter into the covenant.

And then, together we can say:

"The God of peace will soon crush Satan under your feet. The grace of our Lord Jesus be with you." (Romans 16:20)

Amen

MARANATHA